LEARNING TO LEAD IN EARLY CHILDHOOD EDUCATION

Learning to Lead in Early Childhood Education makes a major new contribution to the educational leadership literature in early childhood education. Three sharply contrasting theoretical and methodological approaches are explained in Chapters 2, 4, and 6, each followed by an accompanying case study as a separate chapter. This allows readers to clearly see the relationship between theory, research, and practice, including theory-driven approaches to analysis. By drawing the case studies from three countries – Aotearoa New Zealand, Norway, and Australia, including one involving Indigenous participants – this book allows readers to learn about early childhood leadership policy and cultures in settings with different languages, histories, and national contexts. It will appeal to early childhood center leaders, early childhood education and leadership academics, and postgraduate students in educational leadership interested in the potential of – and for – multiple approaches to leadership research and learning in early childhood education.

JOCE NUTTALL is a research professor at Australian Catholic University, Australia, and a Fellow of the Australian Teacher Education Association. Nuttall's research focuses on professional learning in early childhood education, mainly in Aotearoa New Zealand and Australia, and through collaboration with colleagues in England, Norway, and South Korea.

ANNE B. REINERTSEN is a professor at Østfold University College, Norway. Reinertsen's research focuses on philosophy of education, knowledges of practice, subjective professionalism, academic writing, leadership, materiality of language, and new configurations of research methodologies.

ARVAY HINEMOA ARMSTRONG-READ is an Indigenous scholar and a Mareikura researcher based in Aotearoa New Zealand. Armstrong-Read recently completed her PhD with Monash University, Australia. Her research interests focus on Indigenous knowledge systems, Tupuna mātauranga, Kaupapa Māori theory, Mana wahine leadership, leadership, and the Taiao. Her work has extended to collaboration on research projects with Haukainga, Hapu, and colleagues in Aotearoa New Zealand.

LEARNING TO LEAD IN EARLY CHILDHOOD EDUCATION

New Methodologies for Research and Practice

JOCE NUTTALL

Australian Catholic University

ANNE B. REINERTSEN

Østfold University College

ARVAY HINEMOA ARMSTRONG-READ

Monash University

CAMBRIDGE
UNIVERSITY PRESS

Shaftesbury Road, Cambridge CB2 8EA, United Kingdom

One Liberty Plaza, 20th Floor, New York, NY 10006, USA

477 Williamstown Road, Port Melbourne, VIC 3207, Australia

314–321, 3rd Floor, Plot 3, Splendor Forum, Jasola District Centre, New Delhi – 110025, India

103 Penang Road, #05–06/07, Visioncrest Commercial, Singapore 238467

Cambridge University Press is part of Cambridge University Press & Assessment, a department of the University of Cambridge.

We share the University's mission to contribute to society through the pursuit of education, learning and research at the highest international levels of excellence.

www.cambridge.org
Information on this title: www.cambridge.org/9781316519288

DOI: 10.1017/9781009023207

First published 2023

A catalogue record for this publication is available from the British Library.

Library of Congress Cataloging-in-Publication Data
NAMES: Nuttall, J. G. (Jocelyn Grace), 1961-, author. | Reinertsen, Anne B., author. | Hinemoa, Arvay, author.
TITLE: Learning to lead in early childhood education : new methodologies for research and practice / Joce Nuttall, Australian Catholic University, Anne B. Reinertsen, Ostfold University, Arvay Hinemoa, Armstrong-Read, Monash University.
DESCRIPTION: Cambridge, United Kingdom ; New York, NY, USA : Cambridge University Press, 2023. | Includes bibliographical references and index.
IDENTIFIERS: LCCN 2022056266 (print) | LCCN 2022056267 (ebook) | ISBN 9781316519288 (hardback) | ISBN 9781009010184 (paperback) | ISBN 9781009023207 (epub)
SUBJECTS: LCSH: Educational leadership–Research. | Early childhood education–Research. | Educational leadership–Political aspects. | Educational change.
CLASSIFICATION: LCC LB2806 .N83 2023 (print) | LCC LB2806 (ebook) | DDC 371.2/011–dc23/eng/ 20230208
LC record available at https://lccn.loc.gov/2022056266
LC ebook record available at https://lccn.loc.gov/2022056267

ISBN 978-1-316-51928-8 Hardback
ISBN 978-1-009-01018-4 Paperback

Contents

Figures

Acknowledgments

Thanks are due to the early childhood center leaders who so generously participated in the research reported in Chapter 3:

You are not chosen to be a leader; you are a leader.
Kahore koe ki te whirwhiri he rangatira, he rangatira ke koe

Ko te mahi o te mareikura he ringa atawhai ki te tangata
Ma tona ngakau ki te pupuri te manaaki
Ma tona mana he koha ki te whakanui te tangata
Ma tona tika ki te whakaiti, whakaiti, tika, pono, aroha
Tihei mauri ora.

The work of a true leader is to remain steadfast in their service to one's people
Their heart focused on respect
Their potential is strengthened in their ability to enhance the potential of others
Their integrity is to remain always humble and truthful and kind,
and in doing so balance will be restored and well-being will be present.

We thank Nardo Barnehager (Chapter 5) for their collaboration, especially the general manager and the project leader. Without you the chapter could not have been written.

For the research reported in Chapter 7, we thank the Educational Leaders at Haneul Early Learning Center (this name is a pseudonym) and acknowledge research funding support received from Early Childhood Management Services.

We also acknowledge the steadfast editorial support of Dr. Antoinette White in helping bring this book to completion.

CHAPTER I

The Impetus for This Book: Our Early Childhood Leadership Think Tank

Joce, Anne, and Arvay

1.1 Introduction

Does the field of early childhood education really need another book about leadership? Scholarship about leaders and leading in early childhood education has been available for decades, albeit as a small subfield both of the leadership and early childhood education literatures. The quality of leadership in early childhood education services is now universally recognized as an important factor in the quality of education and care experienced by children and their families (Cheeseman & Walker, 2019). Data from Australia (Australian Children's Education and Care Quality Authority [ACECQA], 2016) show a persistent co-occurrence between good leadership and positive scores on quality metrics for early childhood services.

Less is known, however, about *how* leadership is enacted to promote sound early childhood practice and positive outcomes. What is in the "black box" between leadership and program quality? We may know instinctively if we are working for an ineffective leader, but does this necessarily depress the quality of our practice? These questions remain unanswered because there has been only limited exploration of theories to inform early childhood leadership. This is partly due to the historical reliance on models of leadership for early childhood settings being drawn from contexts, such as schools and business, that are professionally, culturally, and industrially very different to early childhood services (Heikka, Wanaganayake, & Hujala, 2013). A second limiting factor is that the professionalization of the early childhood field is recent, when compared with other sectors of the education profession. This means many new leaders may still rely on polemic and on custom and practice in their development, rather than on approaches that have been tested theoretically and empirically. A third factor is that existing scholarship on early childhood leadership remains strongly attached to interpersonal explanations for effective leadership practice. This is unsurprising, given the nature of the work involved in early childhood education, but this orientation fails to explain how best to educate and support effective leaders. Fourth, and still with science and research on leadership in mind, there is a lack of scientific crossdisciplinary and/or transdisciplinary approaches within the field itself. Structures and traditions of scholarship have prevented interdisciplinary collaboration and theory–practice development for sustainability, social justice, and change in the work of leaders.

This combination – the valorization of leadership as a critical factor in quality early childhood provision and/but a lack of robust theorizing – leaves the early childhood field and its leaders in a paradoxical situation, simultaneously high stakes but vulnerable. Where, then, might we find more robust ways of explaining how early childhood professionals can contribute to autonomous constructions of themselves as professionals and as professional leaders: leaders who are able to reflect critically and control their own practices, based on propositional knowledge that has been incorporated into their own leadership practices, and employ this knowledge to effectively guide the practices of others?

This, in short, is why we have decided to write what we think of as a "metabook" in three parts on leadership in early childhood education, offering different theory and practice perspectives. Our aim is to portray bodies of knowledge to stimulate and decenter the conscience of early childhood leaders and leadership scholars about what they know, enabling them to develop and redevelop their knowledge through points of reference to fit their own experiences. Further, and with reference to the current stasis in understanding leadership that we claim is afflicting the field, we seek to transcend a potential deadlock we see emerging between critique and transformation by opening up possibilities for these to occur simultaneously.

1.2 Why Write a Book about Leadership in Early Childhood Education from Different Theory and Practice Perspectives?

Our response in this book to these challenges is to open up ontologies – how we think scientifically of and about the nature of things – and epistemologies – how we think about knowledge and how it is produced – as resources for leaders. Through this book we aim to recognize the existence of different ontologies and give prominence to the pivotal importance of epistemic conduct in leadership roles and knowledge creation processes. Our strategy is to examine early childhood leadership from within, opening up leadership actions or events for new and expanded visions of social realities, and to position leadership as located in experience, nature, culture, and life, and as a form of collective knowledge and practice. In this way we hope the book offers possibilities for exploring ways forward for the early childhood field. The book is our Think Tank. It describes and theorizes three approaches to understanding leadership in early childhood education, drawn from contrasting theoretical and scholarly traditions: respectively, First Nations' epistemologies from a kaupapa Māori perspective, postrepresentative nomadic process philosophies of education, and cultural-historical activity theory.

The book presents each of these approaches in turn across six chapters. The theoretical basis for each approach is presented in a standalone chapter, followed by a chapter illustrating the theory and methodology in practice through an extended case study. In this way, we want the book to be useful to researchers and academics in its accounts of theory, as well as to teacher educators, professional developers, and practitioners in its accounts of leadership research and development methodologies. In addition to these six chapters, our concluding chapter presents a conversation *between* the approaches that engages with possibilities and limitations for the theories' use in contemporary policy and practice contexts. Hopefully, this will contribute to strengthening interdisciplinarity and open up contestations in early childhood leadership literatures and discourse. We make no claims for the "truth" of the three theories elaborated in this volume. Instead, we take an empirical approach by providing a case-study-of-theory-in-action for each of the background theories. We accept that nothing is neutral, and that no one is neutral; it is therefore necessary to open up our approach to subjective judgment, both from ourselves and, most importantly, our readers. Although we will sometimes give voice to apparently unconscious knowledge processes, we do not seek to separate these from logical reasoning and grounds.

We offer for critique three methodologies for understanding leadership development through the presentation of each theory chapter and its respective case study. But the three methodologies are not entirely separate. Collectively, our approaches are anchored in practices that foster imagination and creativity in professional practice, employing strategies such as narrative analysis, writing, and photography to give expression to the experience of leadership in times of rapid policy development and professional change. We have tried to strike a balance between theoretical, methodological, and empirical aspects of leadership, with empiricism conceptualized in a broad manner to include virtual aspects. Finally, the book offers an international comparison between the cases presented, which are drawn from Aotearoa New Zealand, Norway, and Australia. We wish to contribute to increased mental mobility and learning of leaders in early childhood education, from a standpoint of leadership as emerging and constantly in the making.

1.3   Leadership as Constantly in the Making: Our Think Tank Manifesto

We open, in this chapter, by making transparent the manifesto for our Think Tank. Despite its grand title, we do not see our manifesto as set in stone, but as exploratory, playful, and malleable. It responds to major tensions and challenges we understand to be confronting the early childhood education field at present with respect to the development of leaders and leadership. Although not an exhaustive list, it serves to anchor the chapters that follow in a set of problematics that contextualize policy, research, and practice more broadly than our individual chapters. In summary, our manifesto argues:

1.   That the early childhood field is entitled to reclaim and shape the nature of its professionalism and, indeed, to conceptualize multiple professionalisms
2.   That the early childhood field has its own distinctive body of knowledge, not always represented by government policies that are sometimes bereft of imagination and creativity
3.   That leadership is not a panacea for the "quality crisis" in early childhood education
4.   That the binaries of leaders|followers, leaders|teams, and individuals| community do not serve the early childhood field well
5.   That leadership is not only a form of expertise but a site for making and remaking identity, subjectivity, self-determination, and difference for individual leaders and groups of leaders
6.   That leaders must always contest the nature and effects of change, not just respond to criticisms of continuity
7.   That leadership is an opportunity, and leaders are beholden to do something with that opportunity in relation to the problems of society that reach into early childhood education, including injustice, harmful consumption, and the silencing of diversity in all its forms.

We accept that the assertions of our manifesto are rather gnomic, so we now turn to an elaboration of each of the seven statements, beginning with the nature of professionalism.

1. Reclaiming professionalisms as multiple, complex, and collective.
Early childhood leadership discussions and development are part of – and caught up in – broad and more generic contemporary discussions about evidence-based knowledge creation, professionalization, and/or professionalism. The concept of professionalism has largely grown out from fields like medicine and law, where there have been long-standing efforts to standardize practices to secure quality, equity, and access to services. Given the more "soft," open-ended, and social science and humanities (i.e., relational) nature of early childhood education and early childhood leaders, the field is often characterized as a "semiprofession," or not a profession or professional field at all (Molander & Terum, 2008; Smeby, 2014). This is not necessarily due to any lack of efforts to standardize and secure quality, but a recognition of the complicated nature of theory–practice relationships, and how difficult these are to quantify and measure.

Nevertheless, in a New Public Management and audit-oriented culture, characterized by plurifactual or postfactual (but polarized) public discourse, the concept of professionalism is vital for a field to conquer. Postfactuality describes situations in which people are more likely to accept an argument based on their emotions and beliefs, rather than one based on facts. Being thought of as a semiprofession – or not a profession at all – can easily but imperceptibly be turned into thoughts about unprofessionalism and lack of knowledge, leading to an assumption of poor-quality professional practices. To overcome such postfactual positioning, the field needs to repeatedly achieve perspective and balance through differentiated spaces and affects, supporting educators to escape the tyrannies of perceived opinions, and to avoid "nudging" in particular directions from becoming "shoving" (Reinertsen, 2020). Difference in various situations is always and already classed, gendered, and ethnicized. Professionalism therefore demands iterative, not algorithmic, thinking. It is vital to constantly remind ourselves that evidence might equally work to exclude and diminish justice, as well as be inclusive and just. Clarity, definitions, strategies, and goal orientation can also work to hide, not only reveal. Categories might exclude; the "between" might disappear.

Our Think Tank Manifesto therefore argues for the early childhood field to take back the concept of *professionalisms*, think with it, explore it, and transgress the binaries of qualitative and quantitative, freedom and control, subject and object, real and virtual, individual and collective, body and mind. The plural form of "binaries" here is intentional. We seek to situate a rich and complex view of leaderships in the making, or emergent leaderships, that eschews simplistic notions of "equity," "quality," or "access" within particular forms or models of educational provision. And, as mentioned, we aim to move from views of leadership centered on identity and individuality to a decentered view of leadership, with a focus on collective becomings – professionalisms, rather than individual professionals.

2. Reclaiming the relationship between knowledge and policy-making.
The concept of professionalisms demands that the field claim its distinctive knowledge base, including forms of knowledge expressed as practice. However, early childhood education policy has long been characterized by reliance on particular forms of empiricism that have dictated the nature of valued knowledges for the field. We touch on two of the most enduring bodies of theory here to exemplify how empiricism has not always served the field well: developmental psychology and human capital theory.

Historically, the early childhood education field has drawn extensively on developmental psychology. Although it is a broad field, developmental psychology is principally concerned with the scientific understanding of the relationship between the chronological age of individuals and their behavior across the lifespan, with the study of developmental psychologies of children captured under the overarching term "child development." A variety of binaries (e.g., nature|nurture, stability|change, maturation|experience) characterized the field for decades but, more recently, developmental psychologists have increasingly attended to aspects of culture and cultural norms of child-rearing as important factors in children's development. Criticisms of the influence of developmental psychology on the early childhood field began to gain momentum in the 1990s (e.g., Woodhead, 1999), particularly from scholars employing postmodern and postcolonial theories, who pointed out its Eurocentrism (e.g., Cannella & Viruru, 2003).

The legacy of developmental psychology is important from at least two perspectives when thinking about the relationship between policy formation and knowledge for leadership. First, policies continue to engender a cultural norm of "whiteness" for leaders (Lu & Baker, 2014). We return to this point particularly (but not exclusively) in Chapters 2 and 3, which discuss the experiences of Māori women leaders in early childhood education in Aotearoa New Zealand. Second, it has spawned a raft of "developmental" theories to explain how leaders grow in capability. Examples include Patterson's (2014) four stages of business leadership evolution (expertise, credibility, alignment and execution, strategy) and Freedman and Freedman's (2020) seven stages of leadership development for academic librarians. The issue at stake in relation to such models, and their applicability for early childhood leadership development, is the risk of assuming that there is a developmental relationship between capability and the passage of time.

The reality for many leaders in early childhood education, however, is that they do not have the luxury of time to develop, since they are often thrust into leadership roles "accidentally" (Coleman et al., 2016) or at short notice (Douglass, 2019). Yet policy frameworks assume that those thrust into leadership roles have already reached the higher stages of leadership development. In Australia, the role of Educational (pedagogical) Leader was made mandatory in all early childhood services in 2012, with the expectation that these individuals would know how to lead implementation of curriculum and pedagogy. However, Sims et al. (2015) found these new leaders were mainly focused on improving their understanding of what was *required by policy frameworks* and how to transmit this to others, rather than *critiquing or reflecting on* these frameworks. In other words, new Educational Leaders relied on policy frameworks to define valued knowledge, rather than trusting their own reflexive capacities to connect the frameworks with the needs of the children, families, and colleagues in their immediate sphere of concern.

At the same time as developmental theories have held sway, early childhood education has been increasingly influenced by economic theories. In particular, many contemporary policies in early childhood education internationally have been influenced by human capital theory, a branch of behavioral economics (Tomer, 2016). Once the potential benefits of early childhood education for long-term life outcomes caught the attention of economists, they began to persuade governments and pan-global institutions such as the Organisation for Economic Co-operation and Development (OECD) about the desirability of increased policy attention to early childhood services. These claims rest on analysis of the enduring impact of particular pedagogical models, particularly for children and families defined (also through scientific means such as classification and algorithmic thinking) as "vulnerable" or living in "developing" countries (e.g., Attanasio, 2015). As with developmental psychology, there has been extensive critique of human capital theory with respect to its consequences for education, but much less attention has been paid to its consequences for leaders, teachers, and educators caught up in policy implementation.

From a human capital perspective, it is important to develop leaders' capacity as a necessary step toward development of children's capacities, which, in turn, leads to desirable social and economic ends. This is, however, a highly instrumental and teleological view of leaders (and, inter alia, children) that erases the fact that leaders are also learners with complex needs, capacities, and preexisting knowledges. In this volume, our emphasis is on the professionalisms of leaders in the early childhood sector in a way that assumes they do not need prescriptive definitions of what constitutes "quality" in relation to children and families; rather, they need to be supported to engage with methodologies that can mobilize the rich knowledges *already present* within and among their diverse teams and center families.

Our manifesto, and the way it plays out in this book through theory and case studies, seeks to push back against these developmental and economic positionings in policy regarding the nature and purposes of leadership. However, policy-making anchored in developmental psychology and human capital theory not only exerts its influence at the global and national levels. Local sites, including individual early childhood services, make and enact policies on the basis of desired outcomes and informed by particular bodies of knowledge. Some of these bodies of knowledge are *literally* bodies: the embodied expertise of early childhood educators. In this book we expand on concepts of knowledge, knowledge creation, and meaning-making to challenge how these concepts have been understood historically in policy-making for early childhood leadership.

3. Leadership is not a panacea for the "quality crisis" in early childhood education. A persistent feature of public discourses of early childhood education for the last decade has been the construction of a global "crisis" in early childhood education. The dominant discourse in this construction relates to problems of access and supply, particularly in majority world nations (Best Start, 2016), which are real and urgent. A second feature of global discourse that has also persisted, more commonly in minority world settings, is the intertwining of a crisis of supply with a crisis of quality (e.g., Melamed, 2016). In the Australian context, the highly respected academic Fiona Stanley (2020) has written:

> The enormous economic benefits of *helping women to enter the labour market* has even been measured by the International Monetary Fund, which concluded that "raising female labour force participation rates to male levels could boost gross domestic product by 5 per cent in the US, 9 per cent in Japan, and 27 per cent in India" … Of course, investment in *high-quality* childcare isn't just good for the economy. Giving more parents access to more choices is good for individuals, relationships and, according to a wide range of data collected over a long period of time, for the children themselves. (Stanley, 2020, n.p., emphases added)

This mixing of women's labor market participation, childcare supply issues, and early childhood program quality reflects a central claim of human capital theory: supply in itself is insufficient to provide the economic benefits of early childhood education; programs must also be of high quality. This mix of economic and educational issues underpins a key feature of neo-empirical policy discourses in early childhood education: the pursuit of "what works." In early childhood education, the OECD (Mahon, 2010) has had a major role is sustaining this link between access to services, the quality of services, and the search for panaceas to resolve these ongoing crises.

Effective leadership has been cited as one such possibility and the "quality crisis" discourse has direct implications for leadership in early childhood education. The phenomenon of reluctant principalship that emerged among school leaders over two decades ago (Malone & Caddell, 2000) is now becoming evident in early childhood education. Research highlighting the importance of effective leadership in early childhood services has been mobilized by policy-makers to impose new expectations and accountabilities (often with increased workloads) for center leaders. But now leaders in early childhood education are faced with a paradox with respect to the relationship between leadership and program quality: ineffective leadership in times past is assumed to be a contributor to the contemporary "quality crisis" but, simultaneously, leadership is positioned as one of its solutions. Despite the development of leaders remaining a persistent problem in early childhood education due to the field's lack of robust research and development for leaders, leadership is now simultaneously positioned as part of the solution to improving quality, enhancing professionalisms, and disseminating knowledge.

Our position is to not align ourselves with this putative paradox since it threatens to paralyze center leaders. While acknowledging that millions of women globally face very real problems of access to affordable, appropriate care and education for their young children, we question the nature and purpose of narratives of "crisis" in early childhood education. Roitman (2013) alerts us to the nature of crisis narratives, including their tendency to make a temporal shift from "moments" to becoming an enduring feature of daily life:

> The term "crisis" no longer clearly signifies a singular moment of decisive judgement; we now presume that crisis is a condition, a state of affairs, an experiential category. Today, crisis is posited a protracted and potentially persistent state of ailment and demise. (p. 16)

Roitman articulates the way the term *crisis* also functions to obscure alternative perspectives:

> "Crisis" is a term that is bound up in the predicament of signifying human history, often serving as a transcendental placeholder in ostensible solutions to [a] problem. In that sense, the term "crisis" serves as a primary enabling blind spot for the production of knowledge. That is, crisis is a point of view, or an observation, which itself is not viewed or observed. (p. 13)

Following Roitman we ask: "Who is responsible for creating this narrative?" and "Whose interests are served by this narrative?" Specifically, the cases in this book allow us to ask: "How are leaders positioned in this narrative of crisis? "and "What are the consequences for those leaders?" Evidence presented in the case studies here and elsewhere (Nuttall et al., 2020) suggests that the policy narrative of a quality crisis is driving leaders to take ever greater responsibility for solving problems of the field that are not, in fact, within their control. This strategy of governance, known as responsibilization, mobilizes the positive values and dispositions of dedicated individuals as an alternative to *individuals and institutions together* taking responsibility for the complex problems facing society:

> Responsibilization – namely expecting and assuming the reflexive moral capacities of various social actors – is the practical link that connects the ideal typical scheme of governance to actual practices on the ground. Responsibility – in contrast to mere compliance with rules – presupposes one's care for one's duties and one's un-coerced application of certain values as a root motivation for action (Selznick, 2002). As a technique of governance, responsibilization is therefore fundamentally premised on the construction of moral agency as the necessary ontological condition for ensuring an entrepreneurial disposition in the case of individuals and socio-moral authority in the case of institutions. Neo-liberal responsibilization is unique in that it assumes a moral agency which is congruent with the attributed tendencies of economic-rational actors: autonomous, self-determined and self-sustaining subjects . . . (Shamir, 2008, p. 8)

The relationship between empiricism and policy-making that has led to the responsibilization of crises has failed to resolve important paradoxes that characterize the early childhood field, while leaving leaders and educators vulnerable to enduring problems such as the continuation of poor industrial conditions in some settings. This failure of policy imagination was highlighted during the recent coronavirus pandemic, which positioned early childhood educators as frontline workers, essential for maintaining families' economic activities, without providing them with equivalent job security and health protections (Heffernan & Preiss, 2020). At the same time as they had to manage their own fears for themselves, their families, and their colleagues during the pandemic, they also played a major role in reassuring and educating families (Samuelsson et al., 2020).

4. Binaries of leaders|followers, leaders|teams, and individuals| community. Leadership is messy work, iterative and recursive, and the early childhood field has historically been ambivalent about leadership hierarchies and "the legitimation of positional power to center directors in particular, [which] goes against the natural flow of distributing leadership to others" (Waniganayake, 2014, p. 77). Attempts to explain this ambivalence have invoked the feminized nature of the field (Davis et al., 2014) and "resistance to hierarchical, controlling and instrumental models of leadership that are seen to be at odds with the collaborative, community-based and contextualized work of early childhood education" (Krieg et al., 2014, p. 75). But what if these features are strengths, rather than problems? What if binaries between leaders and followers, leaders and teams, and leaders and the community simply do not serve the early childhood field well – to the extent that early childhood services can be sites for the development of new relationships of leading?

One of the ways in which this is evident in this book is that all three methodologies presented for consideration, despite their ontological differences, rely on concepts of collective thought and practice. Epistemologies anchored in First Nations and feminist scholarship have always held collective knowledge and practice as paramount in theorizing. As noted in point 2, psychology is a late entrant to this way of viewing the world – with the exception of cultural-historical psychology, which derived from the communitarian economic worldview of Karl Marx. This epistemological stance is important for studies of leadership in early childhood education in multiple ways. First, it decenters the personhood of the leader. Identity, skills, subjectivities, and dispositions remain important, but only inasmuch as they exist in a dialectical relationship with the collective whole. Second, epistemologies drawing on collective worldviews lend themselves to recognizing knowledge and skills across teams and communities, contributing to more democratic forms of decision-making. Leaders who know how to foster, identify, and mobilize the distributed professional knowledges available within their teams resist binaries of leader|follower because they recognize that their individual psychology is part of a connected whole that involves the minds of others. This poses its own challenges, of course, but the cases in this book provide three examples of how collective knowledges might be identified and employed in the interests of children, families, and colleagues.

That said, we make no claims for the universal applicability of the methodologies we present. In keeping with our commitment to complex professionalisms, this book deliberately avoids the temptation to provide "recipes" for "effective" leadership. Rather, our starting points are in the on-the-ground experiences of early childhood leaders in diverse cultural, linguistic, economic, and professional contexts. Presenting a variety of cases is not, in itself, sufficient to illustrate and maintain the complexity of leadership for the early childhood field. For this to truly occur, cases of leadership practice need to be understood as existing in tension with one another, as potentially contestable within and across cases, and open to exploration, adaptation, and even rejection. It is in this spirit that we return to the conversation *between* the cases in this book in our final chapter.

5. Leadership as a site for making and remaking subjectivity, self-determination, and difference. Without such contestation of theory and practice standpoints, the field will find it difficult to pursue tricky questions for leaders related to issues such as subjectivity, self-determination, and difference. Following Biesta (2020) we understand education as an encounter *between subjects* that supports people to be *the subject of their own lives*. It is important to note here that Biesta rejects the positioning of subjectivity as a proxy for identity, personality, or the personal; rather, for Biesta, subjectivity is an existential matter deeply connected to one's self-determination.

In the leadership realm, we take this claim to mean that other people are not the objects of leaders but subjects with their own existential challenges, who are appreciated, heard, understood, and even resisted. The necessity for early childhood educators to preserve their psychological wellbeing in workplace relationships (Jones et al., 2019), even as they sometimes fail to achieve it (Hard, 2006), is both an understandable feature of emotionally demanding work and a potential barrier to asking tricky questions. But how can leaders uphold diversity and respect difference if their professional goal is to achieve alignment between subjectivities? This question becomes particularly pointed in relation to upholding the diversity of the early childhood workforce. Despite claims to inclusivity and acceptance, the early childhood field has more work to do in responding to teacher sexualities (Longley, 2020), the rights of teachers with disabilities, and, as we show in Chapter 3, racism (Escayg, 2020) and white privilege.

6. Engaging with both change and continuity. A distinctive feature of neoliberal thought, including its role in much policy formation in early childhood education since the 1980s, is its ahistorical perspective. Each new policy initiative assumes the field can be made anew. Yet early childhood education is a distinctive and long-standing cultural form. As evidence for this claim, we suggest that, despite its local variations from place to place, early childhood educators (and likely also parents) would have no difficulty identifying an early childhood education and care setting wherever they found one. But the effect of recent global and national policy-making has been to imply that this historical form is inadequate, particularly in relation to its contribution to social futures. Like Campbell-Barr (2018), we ask whether questions about the nature of the knowledge base for work in early childhood education, have been silenced in debates about "quality" and "professionalism(s)."

For a long time, knowledge production has been conceptualized primarily as linguistic processes, giving primary focus to the importance of language, hence dialogue as *both method and means*: knowledge, knowledge creation, and meaning-making primarily happen through language. Although it has become fashionable to speak about a sociocultural and constructivist linguistic turn in both science and research, we are also interested in knowledge-creating processes that go beyond speech and thought. We see knowledge creation as material and embodied, in need of an affective component to work, and therefore encompassing experiences that surpasses knowledge-as-language. This demands that we also include the more-than-human aspects of professional life and, through this, give voice to indirect and unconscious aspects of knowledge creation and meaning-making. Our approach is to speak of the *ontoepistemological* turn in science and research. In keeping with the aim of this book to inform future practices of leadership and leadership development, our goals is to act with *foresight*:

> Rapid developments in society might lead to changes in educational structures and contents in the future. In strategic work with education research one should therefore look far ahead, for example through use of foresight *(framsyn),* through including different user groups. Regardless of this, there will be a need for new perspectives and approaches in research about and for the sector in the future. This requires willingness to take risks in research and innovation, which is something the department wishes to facilitate. (Norwegian Ministry of Education and Research, 2018–2019, p. 13; our translation)

For this reason, each of the case studies we present in response to our selected theoretical perspectives engages with the linguistic, the embodied, *and* the affective aspects of professionalisms in an attempt to influence policy, as well as practice, for the field.

The relationship between knowledge and change is a nontrivial question for leaders in early childhood education. Discourses of "quality" and "change" have become deeply entwined in the early childhood field and change, encapsulated in a constant striving for ever-improving quality of provision, has become a byword for leaders. While world events may make us long for stability, we also accept that change is necessary if we are to move away from less helpful aspects of the early childhood education field. Leaders need to be equipped to critique both the continuing form of early childhood provision in local sites, as well as demands for change. Such critique is central to leaders' confident articulation of their professionalism and, without this critique, the field is vulnerable to policy and practice "fads." As will be seen, this book commits to the idea that leadership necessarily involves change and the fostering of change, but also portrays the evaluative capacities of leaders to make judgments in the light of their own historical, local, and practice-oriented knowledges.

7. Leadership as both responsibility and opportunity. Leaders have a critical role in relation to public responses to "wicked problems" of justice, sustainability, diversity, affect, gender, and sexuality. In this book we therefore try to take into consideration both conscious and unconscious aspects of leadership and add value to *weak signals* in knowledge processes and leaderships. We explore how to renew knowledge through open-ended leadership processes that at the same time involve the risk of losing what we currently base our practices on, what we currently value, and what we sense and regard as sensible.

This includes the risk of reopening question of *who knows how to know* in organizations. The future may be echoing into the present, but the question of who knows how to know is forcing us not to close the processes for new generations. We ask how it is possible to stay with the always already unpredictable *foresight in research,* and *in addition,* how it is possible to bring thoughts into reexistence and not to predetermine judgment. This challenges us to rethink the anticipatory nature and power of imagination.

1.4 The Nature and Intentions of Our Think Tank

In contrast to the crisis discourse dominating contemporary policies, our aim is to present some ways the early childhood field might think anew about the development of leaders and the purposes of their work. The book is an invitation to open up and show ontoepistemological and deauthorized knowledge creation processes. As Christie (2009) writes,

One of the most important things might be to upgrade peoples' own experiences, help people to explore their own experiences, make the experiences valid and through this make the carriers of the experiences secure. Secure that they through their lives have experienced something important, something that gives them the possibility to understand related themes, and therefore having the right to speak in several arenas. Maybe the most important role of the social science researcher is to create conditions for people to realize that they know something, thus realize that they are worth something. (p. 53; our translation)

Christie's claims apply to research and researchers as well as to leaders and leadership. As global citizens, we are "sailing the same boat." To make this spirit manifest, this book is a knowledge-creating, ethos-building project, simultaneously anchored in respect, tolerance, and troubles from the start. This kind of realism is our strategy to avoid any incipient temptations from neopositivist approaches to knowledge creation.

With this strategy in mind, we have recast the assertions of our manifesto in the form of questions, which we offer here to readers as one way of navigating within and between the chapters that follow:

1. How is professionalism understood in these chapters? What opportunities do these chapters offer to leaders to imagine a range of professionalisms?
2. How is knowledge conceptualized in these chapters? How do these knowledges reflect or contrast with knowledge as it is constructed by government policies in local leadership settings?
3. What is the relationship between leadership and quality in these chapters? How is quality conceptualized?
4. How do these chapters engage with binaries of leadership in early childhood education? What work is done by these chapters to problematize and help transcend these binaries?
5. What insights do these chapters offer for making and remaking subjectivity, self-determination, and difference for leaders?
6. What is the relationship between continuity and change in these chapters? How is the role of leaders conceptualized as engaging with continuity and change?
7. What opportunities open up for leaders in these chapters? How might leadership in early childhood education engage with the problems of society that reach into and beyond early childhood education?

In combination, the eight chapters in this volume offer, for exploration and critique, three approaches to understanding leadership development in early childhood education. This deliberate search for critique of the three different perspectives and methodologies is what distinguishes this book from other volumes about leadership. It is important for leaders to know about multiple perspectives, different theories, and research traditions and, through this knowledge, become able to interpret and discuss different types of knowledge and knowledge creation in and for leadership. In this way, we hope the book can work as a "metaresource" about leadership for the early childhood field. Our goal has been to present this work at a consistently high level of academic quality, integrating the three sections around a coherent central theme – leadership in early childhood education – with an engaging balance between theoretical/methodological and empirical aspects of the book. For ourselves as researchers – and we hope for our readers – this work was, and continues to be, open, joyful, provisional, provocative, creative, complex, full of curiosity, and anchored in conversations with one another.

CHAPTER 2

Nau mai e Hine ki te Aoturoa a tou tupuna a Tanematuai tiki ai ki roto o Matangireia i a Io Matangaro, i roto o Rangiātea a whata ana*

Arvay

This chapter is based on a doctoral project (Armstrong-Read, 2022) that sought to understand the leadership perspectives of ten Māori women (here-after "wahine Māori") working as leaders in "mainstream" early childhood services in Aotearoa New Zealand. In other words, they were working as leaders outside the cultural safety net of kaupapa Māori that is found in Māori language early childhood centers. The impetus for the epistemological and methodological choices made in the research is crystallized by Pihama (1994):

> Māori people struggle to gain a voice, struggle to be heard from the margins, to have our stories heard, to have our descriptions of ourselves validated, to have access to the domain within which we can control and define those images which are held up as reflections of our realities. (p. 241)

The adoption of kaupapa Māori theory, which is the main focus of this chapter, as the basis for gaining this voice is understood as a form of active resistance to the continuing colonization of wahine Māori who are leaders in mainstream early childhood services in Aotearoa New Zealand. Evidence for this continuation is presented in the case study discussed in Chapter 3.

The chapter begins in the way that is customary when Māori encounter others: a declaration of my whakapapa (genealogy) so that the reader can situate the voice of the author. The chapter then presents a sequence of progressively more refined descriptions of a Māori worldview and how this cosmological and relational worldview influences research, beginning at the broadest level with a brief description of Te Ao Marama, the ontology of the Māori world. The research is then described as a process of engaging with Te Reo Karanga o Matangireia as the tukutuku korero, the spiritual call that motivated and guided the research. This is followed by a description of the emergence of kaupapa Māori theory as a distinct set of principles describing

---

* Welcome women into this world of long-standing light which belongs to our parent who is Tane He who received these treasures from Io whose face is hidden from us

mātauranga Māori (Māori knowledge) that underpins a specifically Māori approach to research methodology. These principles, which draw on both mātauranga Māori and tikanga Māori (Māori cultural protocols) are described, before the chapter concludes with a short description of the study and how it was informed by the sequential knowledge framework of Te Ao Māori, Te Reo Karanga o Matangireia, kaupapa Māori, kaupapa Māori theory, and tikanga Māori. I begin with an account of myself as a Māori woman.

2.1   Toku Moko Kauae

Ma wai e kawe ki tawhiti
Māku e kī atu, e whai, ma mātou ake tonu ake
Who will convey the patterns of my chin to a faraway place?

> In distant lands and times, who will remember me?
> We will. Always and forever.
> (Te Awekotuku, 1991, p. 14)

The moko kauae in Figure 2.1 illustrates my whakapapa and is a symbol that explains who I am. According to Te Ao Māori, one must first introduce oneself, so I begin by explaining my whakapapa and who I am within this research – first as a wahine Māori, then as a wahine Māori leader – and my whakapapa to the early childhood profession.

> He Kākano ahau i ruia mai i Rangiātea.
> I am a seed, descended from Rangiātea.

Figure 2.1   Moko kauae.

I lived in Rangiātea, Te Ao wairua, the spiritual realm before I embarked on my physical journey. My ancient whakapapa reveals the sacred journey that I traversed from the places that are most sacred to our forebears. It was here that I learned of my existence and of my purpose as a wahine Māori, having been formed in the image of atua wahine. These ancient wisdoms provide the sacred threads that bind me to this ancient whakapapa and enhance my identity as a wahine Māori leader in early childhood education. Each line that is etched into my moko kauae conveys the whakapapa of my Te Waiariki lineage, descended from the ancestor of Te Maawe and therefore entitled to the gifts bestowed within Nga Kete o te Wānanga, specifically Te Kete Tūātea, the basket of knowledge relating to spiritual knowledge.

I also descend from the Hapū of Ngāti Hine, formed and led by our female ancestress Hineamaru. Hineamaru was distinguished by her ability to provide shelter and protection for her people in uncertain times. Her name "a-maru" describes her attributes of service, protection, power, and authority. Ngāti Hine wahine are natural leaders, known for their tenacity, strength, strong will, and persuasion.

The third whakapapa I acknowledge is my tuakana (paternal) line, from my ancestor Kawiti. Kawiti was a rangatira who fought against the Pakeha (Europeans) and was one of the few rangatira in Te Tai Tokerau who initially opposed Te Tiriti o Waitangi (the Treaty of Waitangi, signed between Māori tribes and the British crown in 1840). Kawiti was an activist, a political and assertive power that stood with mana. In his ōhākī to my people of Ngāti Hine he cautioned his people to beware of the diminishing relationship occurring between tangata whenua and the crown and the impact of colonization on our people. His ohaki continues to be shared in our traditional gathering spaces even today as my hapū continue to push back and reclaim rangatiratanga (sovereignty) and remind the crown of their obligations to tangata whenua (Māori, literally "the people of the land") in the signing of both Te Whakaminenga and Te Tiriti o Waitangi.

The attributes of each of these kauae rangatira are firmly etched into my moko kauae, and the values that I have inherited through this rich whaka-papa contribute to understanding who I am as a wahine Māori leader in early childhood education and why the topic of leadership chose me.

2.2   The Research

The aim of the research that is partly described in Chapter 3 was to understand the leadership perspectives of wahine Māori and how these are expressed in their everyday practices within "mainstream" early child-hood services in Aotearoa New Zealand. Although the leaders participating in the study were Māori, they did not work in Māori language-based early childhood centers; the research, however, was anchored in epistemological and methodological practices dependent on a Māori worldview.

Leadership is an important decolonizing agenda in early childhood education and particularly in Aotearoa New Zealand. Te Tiriti o Waitangi is the founding document of Aotearoa New Zealand and pro-vides the basis for equity and power-sharing relationships for Māori as tangata whenua. The New Zealand Teaching Standards require all teachers and leaders to have an understanding of and commitment to Te Tiriti o Waitangi demonstrated in their teaching practice. In honoring this com-mitment, educational leaders have the responsibility to enact leadership that reflects Te Tiriti o Waitangi and the perspectives of tangata whenua (Bishop, 1999; Bishop & Glynn, 1999; Fitzgerald, 2003; Fitzgerald, 2006; Smith, 2003).

However, this research sought to not only understand the perspectives of wahine Māori who are leaders in early childhood services but create a space where wahine Māori could tell their stories. Hence the research deliberately sought to offer space where wahine Māori could potentially address ineq-uities they face within early childhood education in Aotearoa New Zealand. In this research kaupapa Māori theory was therefore both an epistemological foundation for the research and a tool to highlight the continuing oppression that Māori experience within institutional structures.

The need to create such spaces and report such research is pressing. There is a growing body of literature concerning leadership in the early childhood sector (Omdal & Roland, 2020; Rodd, 2013; Tamati et al., 2008; Te Kopae Piripono, 2006; Terrell & Allvin, 2021; Thornton, 2019; Waniganayake et al., 2012) and a developing literature concerning Indigenous educational leadership (Fitzgerald, 2006, 2010; Hohepa, 2013; Hond-Flavell et al., 2017; Katene, 2013); however, there is a noticeable gap in the empirical literature regarding who Indigenous leaders are in early childhood education, including how they are accessing Indigenous knowledges. Nicholson (2017) and Fasoli et al. (2007) have argued,

> there is a growing recognition that traditional ways of understanding leadership are no longer appropriate, either for contemporary contexts or for early childhood contexts specifically ... New leadership models acknowledge the importance of these components of leadership, but recog-nise that they do not tell the whole story. (p. 242)

Indeed, Fitzgerald (2003) proposes that a reconceptualization of educational leadership is required, one that includes "the authentication of Indigenous women's voices and a framework that positions Indigenous ways of knowing and leading at the centre of practice and theory" (p. 20). A persistent challenge for wahine Māori leaders in early childhood education therefore is "to assume control over the interpretation of our struggles and to begin to theorise our experiences in ways which make sense for us" (Smith, 1992, p. 33). With Pihama (2001) I argue that "Māori women must speak to and for ourselves. To focus our work on engaging the issues that are important to us" (p. 34) and to ensure these issues are at the forefront of discussions concerning our place as leaders within the early childhood profession. In the next section, I begin by presenting the epistemological principles that underpin Te Ao Marama, which guided the subsequent methodological approach taken in the research.

2.2.1   *Te Ao Marama*

Te Ao Marama is the overarching framework that contextualized the epistemological and methodological approach of the research. Te Ao Marama understands the evolution of knowledge as progressively refined states of consciousness, illustrated in Figure 2.2.

As shown in Figure 2.2, the foundation for the development of knowledge is the act of listening. The wisdom of Te Ao Marama claims that only through one's ability to listen will knowing be attained; then, in attaining knowledge, understanding will follow; finally, through this understanding, enlightenment will be received and true purpose will be revealed. This conceptualization of progression from the act of listening through to

Figure 2.2   Te Ao Marama.

enlightened understanding provides a powerful epistemological basis for research in many settings. Before turning to specific methodological implications of this epistemology, I expand on each of these epistemological *moves*, as represented in Figure 2.2.

Ma te Rongo, Ka Mohio – By Listening, One Will Know. Ma te Rongo Ka Mohio claims that only through one's ability to listen will knowing be attained. As I listened to the literatures of history, anthropology, and previous empirical studies, as well as the study's participants, I was responding to a karanga, a sacred call made by my ancestors past, present, and future, to engage in the research. In attuning myself – listening – to this call, I understood that these ancient knowledge sources would assist me to explore the topic of leadership in early childhood education according to a Māori worldview and answer my research question about the perspectives of wahine Māori leading in mainstream early childhood services in Aotearoa New Zealand.

Ma te Mohio, Ka Marama – By Knowing, One Will Understand. Ma te Mohio, Ka Marama marks the shift from knowing to understanding. This stage brings profound moments of deep reflection and a developing consciousness. This way of knowing was somewhat familiar to me, which led me closer to understanding the Korero Tuku Iho (Mahuika, 2012), the repository of ancient wisdom described in the next section of this chapter, and how and where this would feature within the research.

Ma te Marama, Ka Matau – By Understanding One Will Know. Ma te Marama, Ka Matau is the stage of understanding the challenges handed down by spiritual ancestors and guardians; in my case to use this Korero Tuku Iho (Mahuika, 2012) as a philosophical framework to encapsulate the sacred work of leadership. During this stage I came to further understand the significance of ancestral knowledge and how it could powerfully inform the research. These ancient sources of wisdom (Marsden, 2003) provide the knowledge (Lee, 2009) and learning to better understand the world we live in and to improve the circumstances we face throughout our lives. This affirms that, for wahine Māori who are leaders within early childhood services, this knowledge can serve to assist and shape future leadership practices and solutions.

Ma te Matau, Tihei mauri ora – Through Enlightenment Comes Life, Wellbeing. Ma te matau, Tihei mauri ora is the final stage of knowledge refinement, when enlightenment is received and one's true purpose is revealed in an atmosphere of life and wellbeing. Within this enlightenment phase, the potential of this research to serve and honor many wahine Māori who are leaders within early childhood education finally took the form from which Chapter 3 is drawn.

2.2.2   *Korero Tuku Iho*

Korero Tuku Iho is the repository of ancient and traditional knowledge that allows for a deeper learning and understanding within Te Ao Māori and can be acknowledged as a traditional pūrākau. Pūrākau are framed within "philosophical thought, epistemological constructs, cultural codes, and worldviews that are fundamental to our identity as Māori" (Lee, 2009, p. 1). This ancient knowledge is central to who I am as Māori woman. It allows me to understand and make sense of my everyday life and, in turn, interpret the perspectives of wahine Māori leaders in mainstream early childhood centers in contemporary Aotearoa New Zealand. Lee (2009) advocates for this theoretical and epistemological framing, stating that "pūrākau are a collection of traditional oral narratives that should not only be protected, but also understood as a pedagogical-based anthology of literature that are still relevant today ... which have been constructed to better understand the experiences of our lives as Māori" (p. 1).

Korero Tuku Iho offered the theoretical tools to understand and navigate the complexities in the data to answer the study's research question. Importantly, the Korero Tuku Iho was a gift bestowed upon me by my ancestors to discern the complexities of the data concerning the perspectives of Māori woman leaders in mainstream early childhood centers. For me, this ancient wisdom offered an approach to theorize and make sense of this topic of leadership in our contemporary world and in complex times.

Korero Tuku Iho took the form of a sacred incantation that provided a deeper understanding of the karanga – the call to which I was responding through the research. Like all things in a Māori world, this incantation relied on a whakapapa of spiritual knowledge that encompassed profound messages. The nature of the Korero Tuku Iho is that it protects knowledge (such as the knowledge imparted through the research) and ensures that those who access sacred knowledges do so with humility, respect, and integrity. The specific incantation within this research was an ancient Korero Tuku Iho that speaks to the creation and mana of wahine. It highlights who wahine Māori are as sacred female deities and our whakapapa of wahine atua. According to this ancient knowledge, wahine are endowed with the gifts of our ancestresses and cloaked in the plumes of sacredness. The pūrākau of wahine atua within Te Reo Karanga o Matangireia comprise the attributes of:

- Papatuanuku: unconditional love, sacrifice, ultimate, "Mother Energy"
- Hine-ahu-one: mana wahine, first human, created by the gods, he tapu te wahine

- Hine-titama: changer of destiny, tino rangatiratanga, ownership of future
- Hine-nui-te-po: kaitiaki of the next world, awaiting the karanga, there to greet us.

According to a Te Ao Māori worldview, and transmitted through whakapapa, wahine Māori are born with tapu (sacredness) and mana (authority), and the karanga is a call that only female wahine can perform. The karanga enables the voice of a wahine to open the door that allows the spiritual and physical realms to permeate, so that for a moment in time those worlds converge. Wahine Māori were brought out of the highest temple of the supreme creator and therefore created to be female deities, this being our truest whakapapa. This was the first pattern that was established in the highest heaven of Matangireia, and it was Te Reo Karanga o Matangireia that formed the first sacred karanga. All Karanga descend through this sacred whakapapa, and it is from this sacred whakapapa that the call to leadership is expressed in this research. The karanga is a manifestation of the female essence that evokes the emotions in the hearts of apathetic people to share perspectives and to connect and weave lineages and to bind people both from the realms of the physical and spiritual. The most prominent part of the karanga is to show aroha (love). The karanga comes from within each individual wahine, it springs from her emotions, she intrinsically carries it with her, and it is manifested through the individual emotions and experiences of the woman. The karanga is performed with conviction, integrity, and with love at all times.

There is a place for karanga and it is a discipline that requires attunement to the spirit. When wahine are attuned to wairua (spirituality), the karanga has the ability to pierce the heavens and connect the realms of atua (the gods) with those of our ancestors and loved ones that reside in the heavenly spaces between. When the karanga is performed with the utmost attunement to aroha, the caller becomes the face and the voice of the people. The karanga is an art, a discipline, and a sacred calling that is bestowed upon a person. Hence my karanga of leadership became a calling bestowed upon me to answer the research question. In this way, I became a conduit to represent the wahine Māori leaders and their voices in both a physical and spiritual manner. As I connected to my ancestors, I became attuned to the karanga and embarked on the research.

From these spiritual underpinnings, I now move to the epistemological principles derived from this spiritual realm. I begin by describing the broadest conceptualization of the process of knowledge formation as it is understood within a Māori worldview, one that sees knowledge and spirituality as tightly interwoven. I then outline the principles of kaupapa Māori theory and, as stated at the outset, how the adoption of kaupapa Màori theory constitutes an act of resistance in contemporary research. I then narrow the discussion further, to outline how kaupapa Māori theory informs methodological principles and practices of conducting research with and for Māori in a way that constructs an unbroken line back to the spiritual commitments outlined in the first part of this chapter, including the sacred call to pursue the research.

2.3 Kaupapa Māori – Living Through a Māori Worldview

Ka waiho hei ao marama ki Taiao nei, e Hine e!
To ensure there would be learning and knowledge to light the world

Kaupapa Māori theory has been defined as "the philosophy and practice of being and acting Māori" (Smith, 2012, p. 2) and is the practice of living a culturally aware life through a Māori worldview. As a research paradigm, it can be described "as an attempt to retrieve space for Māori voices and perspectives" (Tolich, 2001, p. 40). As such, the research discussed in this chapter is a means of retrieving a space for wahine Māori leaders' perspectives and voices.

According to Pihama et al. (2002) "Kaupapa is a term derived from key words in the Māori language." *Kau* is referred to as the process of "coming into view or appearing for the first time, to disclose" and *papa* may be interpreted as "ground, foundation base" (p. 32). Nepe (1991) explains that a kaupapa Māori research paradigm is the conceptualization

> of Māori knowledge that has been developed through oral tradition. It is the process by which Māori mind receives, internalises, differentiates, and formulates ideas and knowledge exclusively through Te Reo Māori. Kaupapa Māori is esoteric and tūturu (confirmed) Māori. It is knowledge that validates a Māori world view and is not only Māori owned but also Māori controlled. This is done successfully through Te Reo Māori, the only language that can access, conceptualise, and internalise in spiritual terms this body of knowledge. This knowledge is exclusive, for no other knowledge in the world has its origins in Rangiātea. As such it is the natural and only source for the development of a mechanism which aims to transmit exclusively kaupapa Māori knowledge (p. 15).

This conceptualization of Indigenous (specifically Māori) knowledge has led to ongoing debate about what distinguishes it from other claims about forms of knowledge. Wilson (2001), for example, argued that a kaupapa Māori research paradigm aligns with other Indigenous paradigms that rely on the "fundamental belief that knowledge is relational. Knowledge is shared with all of creation, this speaks of an epistemology where relationships are more important than a reality" (p. 176). Wilson (2001) also suggested that, by contrast, "Western research paradigms are built on the fundamental belief that knowledge is an individual entity and the researcher is an individual in search of knowledge" (p. 176). However, Mahuika (2008) has proposed that a kaupapa Māori research paradigm "is not about rejecting Pakeha knowledge. Instead it is about empowering Māori, hapū and iwi to carve out new possibilities, and to determine in their own ways, their past, present and future identities and lives" (p. 54). This argument follows earlier claims by Cram (1993), who argued that the "purpose of Māori Knowledge is to uphold the mana of the community." Cram states that Pakeha, on the other hand, "view knowledge as cumulative, whose component parts can be drawn together to discover universal laws" (p. 28). Smith (2021) has continued this conversation, arguing that

> rationality in the Western tradition enabled knowledge to be produced and articulated in a scientific and superior way. As Europeans began to explore and colonise other parts of the world, notions of rationality and conceptualisations of knowledge became the convenient tool for dismissing from serious comparison with Western forms of thought those forms of primitive thought which were being encountered. (p. 170)

In this way, Smith (2021) locates debates about forms of knowledge within "the colonization of Māori culture [that] has threatened the maintenance of that knowledge ... and made it extremely difficult for Māori forms of knowledge and learning to be accepted as legitimate" (p. 175). Smith goes on to assert that Māori knowledge and understandings about knowledge can sit alongside existing Western knowledge. In doing so, she underscores the way debates surrounding culturally specific claims about the nature of knowledge are not only epistemological but political. Specifically, kaupapa Māori Theory can be understood as an emancipatory theory, which not only resists Western theories but seeks to tell the story of colonization and its consequences in Aotearoa, New Zealand.

2.4   Colonization, Te Tiriti o Waitangi, and Research

The history of colonization and its wide-reaching effect on tangata whenua provides a significant context within which to view research and the concept of research in relation to Māori. In 1997 Irwin remarked that

> despite the guarantees of the Treaty of Waitangi the colonisation of Aotearoa New Zealand and the subsequent neo-colonial dominance of

majority interests in social and educational research has continued. The result has been the development of a tradition of research into Māori people's lives that addresses concerns and interests of the researcher's (who are predominantly non-Māori) own making, defined and accountable in terms of the researcher's own cultural world-view. (p. 87)

Around the same time, Durie (1995) was arguing that much research in Aotearoa in the past had failed to demonstrate any benefit to Māori, "so scepticism about the efficacy of research by Māori should not be unexpected" (p. 127). Ongoing evidence presented by Māori researchers (Bishop,1999; Durie, 1995; Smith, 2021) highlights how Māori have been severely misrepresented by traditional Western researchers. As Smith (2021) suggests:

Traditionally research has established an approach where the research has served to advance the interests, concerns, and methods of the researcher and to locate the benefits of the research at least in part with the researcher, other benefits being of lesser concern. As a result, key research issues of initiation, benefits, representation, legitimization, and accountability continue to be addressed in terms of researchers' own cultural agendas, concerns, and interests. (p. 105)

As Bishop noted in 1995, this provided an explanation for the reluctance of Māori to be put "under the microscope" by researchers with little or no reference to who Māori are and their cultural practices or preferences. Pihama (2010) similarly reported that "Māori are concerned that educational researchers have been slow to acknowledge the importance of culture and Indigenous ways of being as key components in successful research practice and understandings" (p. 97). Yet, as recently as 2021, Smith still had to point out that Māori want research to be more mindful of their culture, their practices, and ways of knowing.

Smith (2021) further contends it is essential that the implementation and application of kaupapa Māori continue to serve and validate Māori interest and self-determination. When these practices are compromised there is a danger that Māori are losing themselves as servants to the academic world. A kaupapa Māori approach resists this loss by staying connected to the expertise, advice, and guidance of elders and constantly recalling the purpose of the research. According to a traditional proverb, this is a constant reminder of the necessity to remain focused on what really counts:

He aha te mea nui o te ao, he tangata, he tangata, he tangata
What is the greatest thing in the world, it is people, it is people, it is people

My elders, whanau (family), hapū (subtribe), and iwi (tribe) provided the necessary guidance to inform the research and the means to prevent me contributing to this loss.

2.5   Kaupapa Māori Theory

> Kaupapa Māori theory is the product of a truly literate Māori society and the name of the product is Tino Rangatiratanga.
>
> Walker, 1996, p. 13

Kaupapa Māori theory is a living embodiment of Tino Rangatiratanga, which is "a response to and a critique of dominant Western-European forms of Knowledge which construct Theory. This theory provides an alternative to the dominant dualistic thinking mode of theorising that leads to subjectification, objectification and the creation of the Other" (Walker, 1996, p. 13). Kaupapa Māori theory has developed from a foundation of kaupapa Māori and mātauranga Māori but, as Rameka (2012) points out, "Kāupapa Māori Theory is not new, nor is it a refurbished, refined version of western theories" (p. 47). It is a theory that speaks from within a kaupapa Māori worldview and is consequently a unique philosophical and theoretical framework. This theory is firmly grounded in Aotearoa New Zealand (Pihama, 2001) and

> is not a Theory in the Western sense; it does not subsume itself within European philosophical endeavours which construct and privilege one Theory over another Theory, one rationality over another rationality, one philosophical paradigm over another paradigm, one knowledge over another knowledge, one world view over another world view of the other.
> (Walker, 1996, p. 119)

This is because the purpose of kaupapa Māori theory is to validate (Smith, 2003, 2012) and legitimize Māori knowledge and culture, and privilege a Māori worldview and Māori aspirations. The theory "is motivated by the desire for Māori to know more about themselves, to control the way Māori view the world and themselves, and how the world views and interacts with them" (Smith, 2012, p. 105). Mahuika (2008) insists that kaupapa Māori theory can be described as a "comprehensive framework of knowledge, which entails a range of distinct epistemological and metaphysical foundations which relate to the creation of the universe" (p. 24). Pihama (2010) reiterates that

> Kaupapa Māori Theory provides a cultural template, a philosophy that asserts that the theoretical framework being employed is culturally defined

and determined and maintains that it is intended to ensure a high standard of cultural integrity is retained while critically analysing Māori concerns. (p. 5)

Moreover, kaupapa Māori theory is a method of active resistance to the unremitting continuation of colonization among Māori whanau, hapū, and iwi. Smith (2003) identifies five principles that are crucial to transformation in kaupapa Māori praxis, including "self-determination, validating and legitimating cultural aspirations and identity, incorporating culturally preferred pedagogy, mediating socio economic and home difficulties, incorporating cultural structures" (p. 106), with an emphasis on collective and whanau action, and sharing a collective vision and philosophy. Walker et al. (2006) describe Kaupapa Māori theory as "both a tool and strategy for the empowerment of Māori, and affirming the right to be Māori, whilst constructing a critique of societal structures that work to oppress Māori" (p. 342). Smith (2004) cautioned that, at that time, there was a danger that individuals were "domesticating" kaupapa Māori rather than using it as a tool to empower and transform circumstances that would be of benefit to Māori. Kaupapa Māori theory responds to this critique by constantly seeking to clarify and reaffirm the necessity for kaupapa Māori as a philosophical and theoretical background to examine the perspectives of Māori. Smith (2021) argues that kaupapa Māori theory needs to develop and expand with the new and challenging circumstances that Māori face in contemporary society. As Pihama (2001) reminds us, kaupapa Māori theory is an approach defined by Māori for Māori, drawing on tikanga Māori values and worldviews.

2.6 Kaupapa Māori Theory as a Basis for Research Methodology

Koia i tipu ai te tarahau, te hinana
And so we see this growth and learning continue

Kaupapa Māori methodology is a decolonizing research methodology that was chosen for the research described in Chapter 3 to ensure ethically sound research practices were also culturally respectful and mindful of Māori. Because kaupapa Māori is a comprehensive worldview, it not only describes the nature of knowledge but principles for how knowledge should be produced within a framework of tikanga Māori. These are principles that guide relationships between people, places, and things within a Māori worldview, and which provided sensitizing concepts as a basis for analysis of research data in the project.

2.7   Kaupapa Māori Methodology

In Aotearoa New Zealand, kaupapa Māori methodology has been developed by Māori researchers (Hohepa, 2013; Irwin, 1994; Smith, 2004, 2021) who have worked vigorously within academia to claim a research space for Māori and Indigenous peoples. Smith (2021) explains that kaupapa Māori methodology has developed out of an existing kaupapa Māori theoretical framework grounded in mātauranga Māori; it is an Indigenous research methodology that has often been termed a "decolonising methodology, to serve as a model of social change and transformation that privileges Indigenous knowledge and ways of being" (p. 184). Smith (2021), a pioneer in the development of kaupapa Māori research, asserts that a kaupapa Māori methodology is necessary when research is conducted for and alongside Māori people and communities as this methodology is culturally sensitive and it provides a means to position a Te Ao Māori worldview at the forefront of knowledge production. By applying a kaupapa Māori methodology, I and the other wahine Māori participating in the study had the opportunity to be heard, to speak back, to challenge, and to resist the power of Western research frameworks. As a Māori researcher, kaupapa Māori methodology provides me the opportunity to engage in research that draws upon tikanga Māori principles and affirms my Māori language and Māori worldview, and in turn allows me to articulate meanings within the research.

In keeping with Bishop (2003), I argue that kaupapa Māori methodology is not about being better or replacing other methodologies; rather it is a process of conscientization that provides Māori researchers with a means to enhance, give meaning to, and complement tupuna mātauranga (ancestral knowledge). Specifically within this research, kaupapa Māori methodology validated the work undertaken and highlighted the need to build knowledge and research capacity in the early childhood sector that is of benefit to Māori and continues to develop the aspirations of Māori leaders in early childhood education. Kaupapa Māori research (Smith, 2021) is an important tool for Indigenous communities because

> it is the tool that seems most able to wage the battle of representation; to weave and unravel competing storylines; to situate, place and contextualise decolonizing; to create spaces to provide frameworks for hearing silence and listening to the voices of the silenced; to create spaces for dialogue across differences; to analyse and make sense of complex and shifting experiences, identities and realities; and to understand little and big changes that affect our lives. (Smith, 2021, p. 103)

Kaupapa Māori methodology is framed around principles of tikanga Māori that guide the manner in which research is conducted. These principles have been developed by L. T. Smith (2006) in an attempt to bring ethically sound research practices to the foreground that are culturally respectful and mindful of Māori. Smith (2012, p. 120) provides a set of kaupapa Māori practices to act as a guide for ethical best practice for researchers who may be unfamiliar with a Māori worldview or Māori principles. The seven principles are:

- Aroha ki te tangata (a respect for people)
- Kanohi kitea (the seen face; that is, present yourself to people face to face)
- Titiro, whakarongo ... korero (look, listen ... speak)
- Manaaki ki te tangata (share and host people, be generous)
- Kia tupato (be cautious)
- Kaua e takahia te mana o te tangata (do not trample over the mana of the people)
- Kaua e mahaki (do not flaunt your knowledge).

These principles assist in guiding researchers to behave in specific ways and provide a methodical process that is culturally appropriate for gathering data to inform research.

2.7.1   Tikanga Māori Principles

The overarching principles of tikanga Māori provided theoretical sensitizing concepts that could be woven throughout the research, with each having a specific and significant contribution to the development of knowledge about Māori women's leadership in early childhood settings. Each of the following tikanga Māori principles demand genuine reflection and deep description of how the principles were operationalized. According to Wallace (2018), tikanga Māori principles allow Māori academics the opportunity "to challenge how the Māori worldview is constructed by engaging in discussions that uphold and authenticate Te Ao Māori. Māori epistemology is grounded in kaupapa Māori principles" (p. 175). These tikanga Māori principles (Durie, 1994; Mead, 2016) also can be described as values and principles which are premised upon being correct and true. Therefore, the utilization of these tikanga Māori principles was seen throughout the research to guide and strengthen the research and to ensure cultural ethics and practices were maintained throughout the study.

1. **Wairua.** Wairua is an intrinsic principle of spirituality that encapsulates one's worldview, way of being, identity, and self. Māori have their own unique understanding of wairua that is sacred and intricately tied to the Māori language and the Māori world. Everything within a Māori worldview has a spiritual existence first.

2. **Karakia.** Karakia are Māori incantations and prayers. Karakia are the conduit that connects the physical to the spiritual, to enable and enact a higher level of consciousness that brings clarity and understanding to the work to be done, how it will be done, and who will it do. Karakia are used to invoke spiritual guidance and protection and to increase the spiritual goodwill of an event or gathering, in order to increase the likelihood of a favorable outcome.

3. **Whakaraupeka.** Whakaraupeka is the practice of considering and reflecting deeply upon an idea or notion. It is a process that involves the constant review of ideas to conceptualize and then construct more profound understandings of an idea or topic. Whakaraupeka is heightened through the use of karakia and wairua.

4. **Noho whakaaro.** Noho whakaaro is the process of self-internalization, an ability to be attuned and akin to a deep internal reflection which is enacted over a period of time. Time has no specific end and a conclusion is reached only when the individual has received an outcome or answer for themselves.

5. **Kanohi ki te kanohi.** The principle of kanohi ki te kanohi is undertaken during the hui (meeting). This approach recognizes that information is best shared by Māori in a face-to-face exchange. The term kanohi ki te kanohi therefore describes the communication strategy which is most preferred by Māori when engaging in shared dialogue and discussions. It is important to meet face to face, eye to eye, breath to breath to get a full understanding of the people with whom we engage, to see each other's faces and facial expressions, and to experience body language. Gillham (2000) recognizes that "face to face interviewing may be appropriate where depth of meaning is important and the research is primarily focused in gaining insight and understanding" (p. 11).

6. **Whakawhiti korero.** Whakawhiti korero refers to the manner in which dialogue takes place, maintaining that the dialogue will be a reciprocal exchange, a shared process where people (in this case, participants and the researcher) have time to participate in an exchange in a mutually respectful atmosphere of sharing. Whakawhiti, literally translated, means "to cross over"; in other words, power does

not rest solely with the researcher, who might be recognized as the expert in the relationship. According to a Māori worldview, whakawhiti means there is a shared exchange and that researchers remain humble at all times.

7. **Whanaungatanga.** Whanaungatanga is a tikanga Māori principle that encompasses whakapapa (genealogical links) and focuses on relationships. Pere (1991) describes kinship as the connections that encompass family and beyond the universe: "Whanaungatanga is based on ancestral, historical, traditional and spiritual ties. It forms that strong bond that influences the way one lives and reacts to his/her kinship groups, people generally, the world, and the universe" (p. 26). Whanaungatanga is based on connections and obligations of whanau, hapū, and iwi, which often require an individual to respond to the needs of extended family in various circumstances and situations. Māori are drawn to forming relationships as this is the foundation of a Māori worldview, which asserts that all things are interconnected to all things.

8. **Manaakitanga.** Manaakitanga is intrinsically connected to whanaungatanga and focuses on the nurturing of relationships through reciprocity and care. In a Māori worldview and context, this respect is demonstrated by the way in which guests are looked after and fed. According to tikanga protocols, for Māori there is no time limit to this process. Manaaki means that the door is always open and the well of goodwill will never run dry, no matter how harsh the judgement may be or the suffering which one must go through.

2.8 Conclusion

In this chapter, I have described a sequence from ontology to epistemology to methodology in kaupapa Māori theory; occasionally, I have also pointed to the political nature of kaupapa Māori theory. This theory is not simply a cultural worldview, but an attempt by Māori researchers to resist and overturn the historically accumulating effects of colonization on Māori. As the account in Chapter 3, drawn from the wider study, shows, there is still much to be done to create spaces for leadership in early childhood education in Aotearoa New Zealand that are free from the constant reinscription of colonization on Māori women.

Te Kete Aronui*
Colonization, Racism, and White Privilege in the Lives of Māori Women Leading in Mainstream Early Childhood Centers in Aotearoa New Zealand

Arvay

The research described in this volume's Chapter 2 and this chapter sought to understand the leadership perspectives of ten wahine Māori working as leaders in "mainstream" early childhood centers (i.e., not in Māori medium language services) in Aotearoa New Zealand. In the wider report of the research (Armstrong-Read, 2022), the findings describe the participants' perspectives on leadership in the early childhood sector and the way they draw on their cultural heritage as part of their research, as anticipated at the outset. In engaging with the participants, it became clear that, to varying degrees, they were accessing their ancestral knowledge, with a strong emphasis on using the principles and practices of tikanga Māori to inform and guide their leadership practice.

But the research also illustrated an aspect of the study that was only partly anticipated when the research began: the continuing effects of colonization, racism, and white privilege on the lives of the participants. That the leaders experienced these phenomena is unsurprising, given that they are women of color in a white majority country that is also an ex-colony of the British Empire. However, the clarity and force with which the participants spoke of their experiences and perspectives, within a field that claims to stand for equity, belonging, and wellbeing, eventually became the most powerful aspect of the study's findings. A discussion of the relationship between colonization and leadership for wahine Māori in early childhood education was never intended to be the focus of the study but it could not be ignored: its presence was pervasive in the data. The taonga tuku iho (treasures bestowed) of this chapter is, therefore, a deliberate attempt to highlight the ongoing oppression that acts of

---

* Harmful knowledge

colonization present and the impact of these acts on wāhine Māori who are leaders within mainstream early childhood services.

Chapter 2 outlined a methodological approach to understanding leadership in early childhood education that is specifically grounded in kaupapa Māori theory and in the policy and practice contexts of Aotearoa New Zealand. In the chapter, kaupapa Māori theory is understood both as an approach to understanding how Māori experience their world and as a resource for resisting the harmful effects of that world. This is the dual focus of the present chapter. The first half of this chapter shares the participants' accounts of their experiences of racism and white privilege, which are theorized here as key mechanisms in the maintenance of colonization. The second half of the chapter reverses the analysis to show how the participants were actively resisting racism and white privilege by drawing on the same resources of kaupapa Māori.

3.1 The Nature of Te Kete Aronui

In Te Ao Māori, Whiro is the deity of ever-pervading darkness. I argue in this chapter that Whiro was present to the wahine Māori in the study as the constant, never-ending assault of colonization and its effects. The counterpoint to Whiro is Tane, the deity of light and enlightenment throughout the world. In all matters, there is both dark and light, and in the retrieval of knowledge in the heavenly realms, Tane is constantly encumbered by the feats of Whiro, who is also the god of deceit (Barlow, 1991), and the personified god of evil who has firmly cemented these forces of evil within the ruins of Aotearoa's colonial history.

From a kaupapa Māori perspective, the painful knowledge shared by the participants is retrieved from Te Kete Aronui, the basket of knowledge (Figure 3.1) that contains destructive knowledge, related to darkness, black arts, malevolence, and other knowledges most harmful to humanity. In this chapter, data from the study illustrating this harmful knowledge are presented and organized around three Aho tapu – the first threads that set the pattern of the weaving to follow: colonization, racism, and white privilege. Data are presented that show the ways in which the wāhine Māori leaders continue to be silenced and marginalized by the trauma of their colonial experience within mainstream early childhood services in Aotearoa, New Zealand.

Figure 3.1   Te Kete Aronui.

3.2   Colonization

Catastrophic
Oppression
Lifelong
Opposition
Never-ending
Insulting
Superiority
Assimilation
Travesty
Inhumane
Over it
No more

> Na whiro te koronitanga hei patu
> Whiro is the colonized weapon

A comprehensive presentation of the evidence for the ongoing impact of colonization on the study's participants is beyond the scope of this chapter. Two examples are presented here to illustrate the analysis of colonization reported in the wider study. The first is the way in which the experience of "being Māori" is apparently valorized but in a way that leaves Māori women leaders in early childhood services feeling like failures. The second example relates the experience of shame in not being fluent in the Māori language.

3.2.1 *Feeling Like a Failure in the Workplace*

In hui 1, the meeting held for the individual interviews, several of the wahine described the experience of being positioned as a person who is expected to know everything about Te Ao Māori. Jenna, for example, described how in her center she was expected to be the expert in all things concerning Māori culture, including Te Reo Māori (Māori language):

> As a Māori woman I find that there is an expectation that I know all things Māori including the language. Unfortunately I'm not fluent, [but] I tend to be the go-to person in this area and I do feel as though I have failed my heritage in some ways when I don't know things and that makes me feel really bad. (Hui 1, Jenna)

For Jenna, the expectation that she would be an expert in Te Ao Māori resulted in feeling that she had failed her Māori culture because she was not fluent in the Māori language. Mikaere (1994) argues that

> the most debilitating legacy of colonisation for Māori women is the effect it has had on our perceptions of ourselves. Marginalized by the crown, our roles diminished and distorted by the application of culturally alien values, the end result for too many Māori women has been a negative self-image. (p. 137)

Smith (1992) describes the mechanism whereby the validity and legitimacy of being and acting Māori is taken for granted along with the knowledge, culture, and values. As in Jenna's case, this can position Māori women in challenging spaces that conjure feelings of failure and inadequacy, which in turn have damaging consequences for the manner in which the women feel confident to lead within their early childhood services.

3.2.2 *The Shame of not Being Able to Speak the Māori Language in the Center*

Huhana was also acutely conscious of what it meant for her to be a Māori woman leader who was not able to speak her Māori language. For her, it was "a real challenge":

> A real challenge for me as a leader, as a Māori woman, it has thrown up [is] that I need to learn Te Reo, because [although] I understand some of it, I can't speak it, because I'm not confident to speak it enough and I don't know enough about it and so that's what that challenge has thrown at me, you need to go and learn and so that will be another journey for me. (Hui 1, Huhana)

The erosion of Te Reo Māori as a living language as part of the assault of colonization continues to have an impact on Māori in Aotearoa New Zealand. With the introduction of the Native Schools Act in 1867, Māori were prohibited from speaking the Māori language and were punished for speaking it in playgrounds and at school. This legislation saw generations of Māori families grow up without the Māori language being spoken in their homes. The assimilationist policies of the Native Schools Act resulted in negative attitudes toward the Māori language, which resulted in language loss and near extinction. By 1999, Bishop and Glynn were explaining that the "dominance of monolingualism is so pervasive in New Zealand that the majority culture is unable to accept cultural diversity as a positive feature that those other people bring to the nation state" (p. 12). Huhana's experience parallels that of Jenna, who described herself as "embarrassed":

> I actually feel quite embarrassed that I don't have the reo, so I try not to talk much, I do feel a sense of embarrassment, it's been a painful experience and a challenge. (Hui 1, Jenna)

For both Huhana and Jenna, their lack of fluency in Te Reo Māori is more than a challenge. It is felt as a deep sense of loss that affects their self-esteem and confidence in feeling worthy and able to connect to their true selves as wahine Māori. Their pain and embarrassment speak to the way historical acts of colonization continue to subliminally reside within the minds of those who have been most oppressed, even if they are from generations of Māori born after the repeal of the Native Schools Act in 1867.

Te Reo Māori is more than just a language. Like all languages, it is through Te Reo Māori that a Māori worldview is best understood. One of the consequences of colonization, as described by Huhana and Jenna, is to deny access to the deep and rich repositories of knowledge informed by a Māori worldview. The consequences for Huhana and Jenna are tarnished experiences as wāhine Māori, leaving each of them with negative attitudes of self-worth, feelings of embarrassment, loss, and pain due to not knowing their language.

3.2.3 Shame, Failure, and the Colonial Project

The study's participants all carried considerable responsibilities as leaders in their early childhood centers, yet spoke of the struggle to make sense of their lived experience in contexts where they had diminished cultural resources of language and ancestral knowledge available to draw upon within their leadership roles. The embarrassment and loss of confidence they described illustrate one of the supreme achievements of the colonial project, that of reaching the point where wāhine Māori do not have to be actively marginalized because they are now marginalizing themselves from within. The study's participants described their lack of access to cultural resources as a personal failure and source of shame but, in fact, it is a consequence of the ongoing effects of colonization that are undermining their dignity and authority as wāhine Māori. Two key mechanisms for the maintenance of these effects are racism and white privilege.

3.2.4   Racism

Radical
Assimilation
Colonial holocaust
Internal extermination
Suffering
Masking

> Na whiro te kaihanga o te tukino tangata
> Whiro is the god of deceit and the composer of all racism

Racism can take many forms. Spoken or unspoken it is woven into systemic and institutional structures in subtle ways that continue to marginalize and oppress individuals. Evidence from the study suggests Māori women who are leaders within mainstream early childhood services are all too familiar with the construction of racism and the manner in which this plays out in their role as leaders. Three entry points for understanding how racism maintains the colonial project are presented here: self-silencing, blatant racism, and knowledge appropriation.

Self-silencing. Many of the participants spoke about racial tensions and biases that they have had to contend with during their careers as leaders in mainstream early childhood services. Some were more confident in articulating examples of racism and prejudices than others. But often the participants didn't have the words to describe what they had experienced, conveying it instead through tears and deathly silences that contained their experiences of hurt and trauma. Hineira and Kiri each described the experience of staying silent and absorbing experiences of racism:

> There were moments when I just shut down and refused to talk about the hurt because I was over it and I guess it was a way of coping with being shut out and being pushed aside. (Hui 2, Hineira)

> You know, sometimes the hurt was so deep I put it right to the back and
> didn't talk about it until now and then it's still hard for me to talk about
> the tukino. (Hui 2, Kiri)

Both of these wahine expressed their difficulty in talking about the hurt
that came about through racial labeling. These findings align with research
by Ritchie (2008, 2014) that suggests that research concerning Māori and
racism in Aotearoa is an ongoing decolonizing project. Ritchie's research
describes kaiako (teachers) in early childhood services in New Zealand
expressing their difficulty in verbalizing resistance to racism, and finding
their efforts to call out racism extremely confrontational and stressful.
I suggest that, for wahine Māori, it is almost impossible to articulate the
racism that had occurred for them since, by definition, they are already
working in spaces where it is unsafe to be Māori and therefore unsafe to
point to the trauma they have experienced. Consequently, they decide to
keep silent.

Blatant racism. During the study Ruihana shared an account of a
blatant racial experience that left her feeling devalued and belittled, even
though the eventual outcome of the story was a hard-won triumph for
Ruihana. As a high school student, a teacher had demanded of her:

> "What are you going to do . . . when you leave school?" I said, "I'm going to
> be a teacher." He said to me, "I'll laugh the day when I see that . . . you're
> going to be nothing." You know, that was a wero [provocation] to me.
> I said to myself, "I'll show you." And, you know, when I was in [the
> University of] Waikato I Mahi Ahau Tōku Bachelor of Ed[ucation course]
> I was asked to do a guest lecture and I said, "Okay." [The lecturer] said,
> "It's only a little class . . . they are all teachers." And I got to take the class
> and the exact teacher that said what he said to me [in high school] was
> sitting in my class. I could see him really looking at me, and I said to myself,
> "Yeah mate, it's me, it's me." He [said] to me, "Your face is very familiar to
> me." "It should be," I said, "You used to be my teacher." [He said], "You're
> not. . . . . . ?" I said, "Yes I am sir, and I'm a teacher. Who ever thought you
> would be my student? That's me. Remember you said to me [I would]
> never get out of Mangakahia, and here I am Sir." He was whakama
> [ashamed], he probably regretted his words. That was really funny, the
> universe just turned on its head. (Hui 1, Ruihana)

Rihi also described experiences of blatant racism and how they made
her feel:

> There were a lot of experiences when I felt people takahi and stamping on
> me, I think it was a racial thing and sometimes I would think, *I'll just let
> that pass because there's no sense in me carrying that around.* But I don't

forget, this is something so deep, and sometimes I think it's best to leave things lying. (Hui 1, Rihi)

As with Hineira and Kiri, the experience of racism was paralysing, so that the depth of hurt caused by racism hampered Ruihana and Rihi's ability to process racist experiences, leaving them feeling it was best left unspoken. Such paralysis is intimately bound up in racist controlling behaviors of power. Fitzgerald (2003) suggests that wahine Māori who are leaders are often silenced through power relations within education, and Smith (2021) argues that, in Aotearoa New Zealand, wahine Māori have been subjected to constraints of colonization that have undermined their ability to withstand ongoing racism other than by suppressing the desire to respond:

> I remember a place where I was working and the things they used to say to me, they even asked me what I was doing here once. I thought to myself, *I don't want to be here and I really don't want to associate myself with people and places like this.* I felt I didn't have a place here. I hated working here and the only reason I stayed was because of the children and what was important to me was the people that I surrounded myself with. (Hui 1, Hohi)

Bishop and Glynn (1999) explain that racism is the framework that best serves a monocultural elite. As Ani explained,

> Undermining us as Māori always happens all the time, and sadly this will happen with my children. You know, I want my daughters to grow up as strong young Māori women knowing who they are and their identity, and not to let anybody, even for a split second, try to diminish that or take that away from them. (Hui 1, Ani)

Knowledge appropriation. A third racist mechanism experienced by the participants related to the use of Māori knowledge. Ruihana argued that *Te Whāriki*, the New Zealand early childhood curriculum (Ministry of Education, 2017) was a living form of epistemological racism. She articulated that the knowledge embedded in *Te Whāriki* was not new or innovative and had been colonized according to the dominant (Pakeha-European) culture. She believed that the Māori knowledge incorporated into *Te Whāriki* should be recognized within traditional sources of knowledge in early childhood education and validated as such:

> I remember when *Te Whāriki* came out I was a bit anti, not anti what was in it but what was behind it. This is the way our people have taught mai rano, but you only acknowledge it now because you put it in your little framework in a little book and all of a sudden it is new-found knowledge, when this is something that our people have taught for many generations. So even though I love the kaupapa [purpose] of it, we don't even need that

book, we need to recognise the knowledge that each person brings more than a tohu brings, it's even more valuable. (Hui 2, Ruihana)

I understand Ruihana to be saying that Māori women as leaders in mainstream early childhood services are all too familiar with the manner in which knowledge is colonized and then repackaged. This appropriation of cultural knowledge is a form of epistemological racism, a mechanism of the colonial project that shapes legislation, government policies, and educational practices. The consequence for wahine Māori who are leaders in early childhood services is a lived reality of knowledge appropriation.

3.2.5   White Privilege

White
Historical
Intergenerational
Trauma
Extermination

Privilege
Resistance
Invisible
Visible
Impose
Life long
Extinguish
Genocide
Extinction

Na whiro te tuakiri o te tukino tangata
Whiro is the god that perpetuates oppression

White privilege can be broadly defined as the advantages available to white people who live in societies that are founded on inequalities arising from the concept of "race" (a purely discursive construct that has no basis in biology). Like racism, white privilege is enacted through signature mechanisms of power and oppression. Four of these mechanisms are described here: denial of one's status as first people; lack of accommodation of cultural expectations; deliberate ignorance about community norms; and superficial acknowledgement of biculturalism.

Denial of the status of tangata whenua. Māori were the first people to inhabit Aotearoa New Zealand and their sovereignty is explicitly acknowledged in Te Tiriti o Waitangi. Yet, as Ani explained, there can be a constant challenge in toiling to have the Māori people and culture recognized and affirmed as tangata whenua:

> It's a challenge when our place as tangata whenua is not recognised so we have to be this other way so people will get it. But inside of who we really are is this Māori person that wants to be a Māori. But sometimes it's difficult because they don't want to know or even begin to understand ... [The need for] reaffirming our identities and the lack of recognition for us as Māori happens all the time. (Hui 1, Ani)

That leaders such as Ani have to constantly reassert their status as tangata whenua in the twenty-first century explicitly dishonors obligations under Te Tiriti o Waitangi early childhood education, which are enshrined both in treaty and in law. Here again we see the power of the project of colonization, which has made Māori primarily responsible for the constant attention and interrogation needed to ensure cultural amnesia does not pervade early childhood services.

Contemporary mainstream early childhood services have developed out of a history founded upon early colonial ideals and values, and mainstream early childhood services, particularly where the majority of teachers are Pakeha, may maintain an entrenched Western worldview. Gordon-Burns and Campbell (2014) suggest that mainstream early childhood services continue to enact forms of colonization by exclusively operating from a "monocultural monolingual paradigm, in which the dominant language for transmission of ideas and everyday conversation is English, and where the culture within the centers is organized around Western beliefs and practice" (p. 22).

Bishop and Glynn (1999) further note that

> because monocultural Pakeha teachers continue to dominate the education system and because these teachers, being part of the dominant majority, did not perceive that they themselves had a culture or a particular way of viewing the world, they promoted the "non-culture phenomenon." This meant that teachers unwittingly and uncritically promoted their own culture as the standard to which others were to be compared (p. 40).

The subtle paradox of the "non-culture" phenomenon allows for a dominant culture of whiteness to determine practice within mainstream childhood services, despite mandatory requirements to operate as bicultural institutions in Aotearoa New Zealand. The positioning of whiteness as "normal" not only renders white privilege invisible but renders everyone who is not pakeha as "other" kinds of people. The consequence for Ani as a wahine Māori leader is to hamper her ability to practice and draw on her

Māori worldview. Ani articulates a longing to be recognized as tangata whenua, even in the context of a legal commitment of partnership between tangata whenua and the crown.

Lack of accommodation of cultural expectations. Many First Nations observe rich and strict protocols related to ongoing cultural life as well as key events such as funerals. Ani described the challenges of what it is like to be a Māori woman having to navigate her role as a leader as well as continuing to give of herself to her whanau and community:

> You know, I get it. As Māori women we have to juggle the mahi [work], our whanau, our kids, our extended whanau and then if you're involved in the marae [traditional village or meeting place] and then there's the hapū [extended family] meeting. So when you say, "I don't know if I can participate in the research because I've got too much on," that's the lived reality for us as Māori, it's a contention that we all face. (Hui 1, Ani)

The normalizing of Western practices constitutes the core of white privilege. McIntosh (1989) describes this as an "invisible weightless knap-sack of special provisions, maps, passports, codebooks, visas, clothes, tools, and blank checks" (p. 35). Yet, as Meadows (2002) points out, "whiteness carries the weight of a long history of oppression and institutional racism" (p. 36). This is further noted by Rains (1998) who asserts that

> this privilege of Whiteness trivializes the substance and weight of the intertwined histories of Whites and people of colour, and ignores the poor quality of treatment that many people of colour encounter, and denies many people of colour their right to their respective identities, while it safeguards how the individual white person engaged in this response may appear in the name of political correctness. (p. 93)

As Ani explained, Māori women finish their paid work and go home to commitments and responsibilities that reach beyond their nuclear families, to a family structure that encompasses an extended whanau and even commitments that encompass broader tribal responsibilities.

Deliberate ignorance. Hineira was highly articulate about overt acts of white privilege that she had encountered while working in her early childhood service as a leader. One example was of the way her work was characterized as being within "a marginalized community." In other words, her work with Māori children and families was treated by her wider employing organization as a stigma:

> We are in a marginalised community and lots of people don't like to admit that. We have difficulties that lots of other communities don't, and they wouldn't even have an understanding of that. All of the children that are

enrolled here are all Māori, our staff are all Māori. We are different from all
the other kindergartens. We . . . are those odd cousins on the outside [that]
people want to learn about and be a part of but they also have a fear of us
as well. (Hui 2, Hineira)

Hineira was also attuned to some of the advantages of this outside status:

We can be quite autonomous here as well, we can carry on and do our own
thing because they can't compete or argue with things, because we have to
be able to do things the way we do stuff here and they can't argue with it, so
that's who we are in our kindergarten. (Hui 2, Hineira)

In her awareness of the mechanisms of racism, including white privilege,
Hineira reflects Frankenberg's (1993) assertion that "whiteness, as a set of
normative cultural practices, is visible most clearly to those that it excludes
and to those to whom it does violence. Those who are securely housed
within its borders usually do not examine it" (p. 229). As Giroux (1998)
notes, "white society lacks the vocabulary to contest the status quo. There
are not even adequate words to address Whiteness and its many layers. As
long as there is a lack of discourse related to Whiteness, it will retain its
sense of being everything and everywhere" (p. 35). My conversation with
Ani led me to believe that white privilege can be a means for organizations
to avoid engaging with services that are somewhat different to what their
normalized worldview is. By labeling the setting for Ani's center a "marginalized community," Ani's employer excuses itself from the obligation to
understand how to best support Māori children and families.

Superficial biculturalism. For white colleagues and employers in early
childhood education in Aotearoa New Zealand, the alternative to fully
engaging with Te Ao Māori is to take a "tick the box" approach to
culturally responsive teaching practices. This is not an option for wahine
Māori leaders. As Hineira explained,

So we have to make sure that we have that accountability to our governing
bodies, but also its about making sure that we do not comprise kaupapa
Māori. So our strength in our kindergarten is . . . [that] we don't compromise just because we have a tick box that we have to meet accountability for
other agencies or our management. (Hui 2, Hineira)

For Hineira it is paramount that she does not compromise the cultural
integrity of the service in order to meet organizational requirements that
take the form of superficial compliance with bicultural principles. Given
that Hineira is leading in a mainstream early childhood center, her center
is likely to be an exception in this regard. Few mainstream early childhood
services privilege the Māori worldview or even use the Māori language as

the language of instruction. Instead, Māori language may be spoken as an absolute minimum requirement for compliance purposes, rather than as an integral part of the heritage of Aotearoa New Zealand to which all New Zealand children are entitled.

To summarize this chapter so far, I have suggested that racism continues to maintain the original project of colonization in Aotearoa New Zealand and that mainstream early childhood services are sites of struggle where wahine Māori who are leaders have to constantly navigate the continuing effects of colonization. The data presented in this chapter suggest that racism and white privilege are lived realities for wāhine Māori in both their personal and professional lives in Aotearoa New Zealand and that racism is a constant disruptive force in their professional lives within mainstream early childhood services.

In the remaining sections of the chapter, I turn again to kaupapa Māori theory to show how it serves not only to analyze the effects of the colonial project but to enable resistance and resilience for wahine Māori leaders in early childhood education. In the discussion that follows, I first summarize insights from Te Kete Tūātea, the basket of knowledge that pertains to the spiritual realm. I outline, in turn, the participants' recourse to the spiritual concepts and practices of tapu (sacredness), mana (authority), and wairua (the spirit). I then summarize the study's findings in relation to the second basket of knowledge, Te Kete Tūāuri, which relates to knowledge inherited from ancestors. In relation to this second basket, I describe concepts of whanaungatanga (relationships), manaakitanga (hospitality), and aroha (love).

3.3   Te Kete Tūātea

Mauria mai nei, Ko te Kete Tūātea
Bring the knowledge encapsulated in the spiritual basket

Te Kete Tūātea is the basket of knowledge pertaining to spiritual knowledge. Drawing from this basket of knowledge, the wahine Māori spoke of how they were able to access particular forms of spiritual knowledge anchored in their Māoriness. Moreover, they spoke of the distinctively Māori quality in their perspectives on leadership. When they talked about leadership, they expressed drawing deeply on their Māori worldview to articulate leadership and, in doing so, drew upon tikanga Māori principles (tapu, mana, wairua) to describe their leadership and how it was enacted.

3.3.1 Tapu

Tōku tapu, Tōku pū Mareikura e
My sacredness is in knowing my sacred and divine purpose

Ancient karakia (prayers) describe how wahine Māori descend from the divine whakapapa of Hineahuone, the first female deity (Murphy, 2017). According to tupuna mātauranga, wahine are born with and carry the innate spiritual gifts (Murphy, 2017; Te Awekotuku, 1991) found within Te Kete Tūātea. The wāhine in the study explained how they thought about and applied tapu in ways that were authentic and meaningful for their leadership roles. This occurred in two ways. First, when wahine Māori understand their own tapu, they are conscious of their own sacred and divine purpose as a source of confidence to assert their passion as a leader. The participants saw this understanding of tapu as enabling them to express themselves in their roles as leaders, and to support children and families to recognize their own tapu. Second, the wahine shared that, through knowing their tapu, they recognized leadership potential in others. Halpern et al. (2021) discuss this idea in their research, finding that "everybody has the capacity to be a leader, which implies an inclusive nature of leadership" (p. 673).

In practice, the participants saw their tapu as a sacred calling that meant their leadership was never about having a title or being identified as the sole leader in charge. Clark (2012) contends that hierarchical forms of leadership have historically been resisted by early childhood practitioners because they are "averse to being in a position of dominance" (p. 16). However, for the participants in the study, their anti-hierarchical stance was grounded in their sacred nature, inherited from birth.

3.3.2 Mana

Tōku mana, tōku mana Motuhake e
My power is my inherent prestige

Standing in their mana was defined by the wahine Māori as knowing their Māori language and having a connection to their ancestral whakapapa and genealogical links. They also conceptualized their leadership as a form of mana, underpinned by acts of humility and able to serve and honor their people. Katene (2013) stipulates that mana is enacted and heightened through one's service to people. This recognizes that, as the leader serves the people, the mana that is inherently gifted to the leader at birth is further enhanced. In her doctoral study, Wirihana (2012) made a similar finding in relation to thirteen wahine Māori leaders and their life experiences. Wirihana's study revealed that the women, who were influential leaders in their communities, were taught very early in their careers that serving their communities was essential to being an influential leader.

A further aspect of mana identified by the early childhood education wahine Māori leaders related to tensions they grappled with regarding the language of leadership and their titles as leaders. Here the wahine preferred to use the title "enabler" as a more appropriate term to define their leadership. Using the title of leader was, in their eyes, a term that diminished their mana and was therefore a form of disrespect. Mikaere (1994) explains that

> mana embodied in self and other is as much about authority as it is about power. Consideration of mana in processes of encounter emphasises the ability to potentially diminish the mana of others if it is ignored or disregarded. What this suggests is that mana is an integral component of interpersonal relationships that requires the consideration of accountabilities extending beyond that of a particular discipline. (p. 5)

3.3.3 Wairua

Wairua was described by the wahine as being pivotal and fundamental to their work as leaders. Some described spiritual knowing as a type of conduit that enabled them to connect to their spiritual ancestors to ensure guidance and security in their work as leaders. For others, wairua helped them connect to their higher spiritual and emotional selves. By connecting to this higher level of consciousness, the wahine explained they were better able to manage themselves and express their feelings and needs. Marsden (2003) explains that Māori have their own unique understanding of wairua that is sacred and intricately tied to the Māori language and the Māori world. Everything within a Māori worldview has a spiritual existence first, intimately woven within and across the aeons of Māori existence.

From a kaupapa Māori perspective, wahine who choose to work in isolation, or ignore the use and guidance of wairua within their leadership practice, run the risk of endangering themselves or losing themselves to worldly solutions to guide their practice. Douglas-Huriwai (2012) reminds us that

> Māori culture is enormously spiritual ... The risk we run if we approach our spirituality in a passive manner is that we reduce these most intimate of times into little more than a role play, a performance with no substance.

This means that we have an obligation as Māori to become more spiritually aware. (p. 102)

In this conceptualization, wairua becomes embodied as a pedagogical practice, pivotal and integral to wahine Māori and their work as a leaders. Pedagogical leadership within the literature is described by Heikka and Waniganayake (2011) as leadership for learning which focuses on pedagogy and improving practice. The literature on pedagogical leadership asserts that this approach has the capacity to transform leadership and assist leaders to navigate dynamic learning spaces and curriculum. There is a growing body of literature (Heikka & Waniganayeke, 2011; Ord et al., 2013) within the early childhood sector concerning pedagogical leadership and the work associated in improving teaching practice and creating new areas of professional growth and leadership. However, there are few notions of pedagogical leadership that remark on the notion of wairua or begin to discuss spirituality as a legitimate dimension of leadership that contributes to quality programs for children and families.

3.4   Te Kete Tūāuri

Te Kete Tūāuri is the basket of knowledge pertaining to ancestral knowledge. In drawing from this basket of knowledge, the participants spoke about the way they were able to access and draw upon tikanga Māori principles to enact their leadership practice. As explained in Chapter 2, tikanga Māori principles derive from kaupapa Māori; furthermore, they have a distinct epistemological and metaphysical foundation related to the creation of the Māori universe. Leadership for the women in the study included being able to draw from their Māori world to apply tikanga Māori principles to their work as leaders. This, in turn, built confidence in normalizing these principles within their teams.

Rameka (2012) argues that re-entering the world and being Māori within today's context requires skilful navigation of drawing from past ways of knowing and being. Rameka notes that ways of being and knowing provide kaiako with cultural tools which assist them to navigate and make meaning of their work within early childhood education. Smith (2021) further contends that these ways of knowing and being are "about reconciling and reprioritising what is really important about the past with what is important about the present" (p. 39). In this last part of the chapter, I summarize the use of three aspects of tikanga Māori that featured in the study's findings: whanaungatanga, manaakitanga, and aroha.

3.4.1   Whanaungatanga

He aha te mea nui o tenei ao, he tangata, he tangata, he tangata
What is the greatest thing in this world, it is people, it is people, it is people

Whanaungatanga is a tikanga Māori principle which was invoked by the wahine to convey the importance of relationships in their leadership. Whanaungatanga responds to the importance of connections with people and places (Bishop, 2005). It encompasses the family and extended networks and relationships, and the manner in which these relationships are developed, managed, and sustained. This principle also involves caring for and working harmoniously with people to achieve common goals, and using relational strategies such as fostering tuakana-teina (an elder–younger pedagogical relationship).

Most of the wahine in the study discussed whanaungatanga as the foundation for everything they did as leaders. Whanaungatanga was noted by the wahine as being so pivotal to their upbringing within a Māori worldview that they were now able to use as a tool to conceptualize their own leadership perspectives and experiences within mainstream early childhood services. In particular, they noted that whanaungatanga was about creating spaces where families could have a sense of belonging and find greater connection to one another and to the people working in these spaces.

3.4.2   Manaakitanga

Nou te rourou, naku te rourou, ka ora te iwi
With your basket, and my basket the people will be well

Manaakitanga is fundamental to the collectivist nature of the Māori worldview and is synonymous with reciprocity. While whanaungatanga indicated the importance of relationships for these leaders, manaakitanga played a key role in connecting and developing reciprocal and respectful relationships with children, families, and their colleagues. Manaakitanga means that leadership for these wahine was enacted through acts of kindness and respect. The sharing of food, an important aspect of manaakitanga, was discussed as a culturally appropriate practice to sustain and develop these relationships. Manaakitanga was further described in terms of hospitality and depicted as the ultimate level of respect that one shows to visitors (Barlow, 1991). The wahine concluded that manaakitanga was also evident in working with a spirit of generosity, not just in the exchange of physical objects. Manaakitanga could be incorporated into their leadership practice at a personal level through acts related to time, honesty, and vision.

3.4.3 Aroha

E iti, noa ana, nā te aroha
A small ordinary thing, begotten by love

Aroha, although historically translated as "love," is a complex concept within a Māori worldview that is also synonymous with reciprocity and selflessness. The wahine Māori, however, when describing their use of aroha as part of their leadership practice, noted that aroha was only present once whanaungatanga and manaakitanga had been enacted. One of the leaders noted that, when aroha not present in the work of a leader, the leader becomes detached from what matters most in their career. She suggested that aroha must be paramount in the practice of a leader if they are to be effective in all that they do.

3.5 Conclusion

This chapter began by illustrating, through their own words, how the experiences of wahine Māori who lead in mainstream early childhood centers in Aotearoa New Zealand reflect the continuing effects of colonization, mobilized through racism and white privilege. In the second half of the chapter, as a counterpoint to these painful stories, summaries were presented describing how these early childhood center leaders drew on principles and concepts of kaupapa Māori and tikanga Māori to inform their leadership.

I conclude with three observations. First, in examining how leadership is conceptualized and expressed in early childhood education research, there remains a paucity of studies related to First Nations peoples and a lack of recognition of Indigenous principles as contributors to effective leadership. Rameka (2012) suggests more work is needed to reclaim and reframe questions about who has the power to define leadership, whose truths are being reflected, and how are these truths are constructed.

Second, I suggest it is time for the early childhood field in Aotearoa New Zealand and elsewhere to make a serious reckoning of the ongoing harm perpetrated by racism and white privilege. The participants in this study described their perspectives of failure and loss in the context of a national early childhood policy framework that claims to incorporate the principles of the Treaty of Waitangi, but which some saw as tokenistic or – even worse – as cultural appropriation. The participants' feelings of shame are all the more disturbing when we remember that these women are in significant positions of leadership in licensed early childhood services.

Third, I observe the way the study's participants had adopted tikanga Māori principles not only as a framework for their leadership, but to give legitimacy to their perspectives as wahine Māori. For them, kaupapa Māori is a source of strength and resistance. Smith (2021) calls for a time when the "validity and legitimacy of being Māori and acting Māori, and being Māori is taken for granted. Māori language, culture, knowledge and values must be accepted in their own right" (p. 13). For the participants in this study, that time is yet to arrive.

CHAPTER 4

Leadership as Change
Immanent Knowledge Practices for Emergent Educational Leaderships and Organizational Learning

Anne

> Philosophy is the theory of multiplicities, each of which is composed of actual and virtual elements. Purely actual objects do not exist. Every actual surrounds itself with a cloud of virtual images. (Deleuze, 2002a, p. 148)

This chapter is a critique of discursive productions of educational leadership policies and subsequent programs. It is a critique of the current features and push in education and leadership toward continuous assessment for continuous improvement; education and leadership as personalized learning; growth-mind-sets as a policy mandate; and the discursive moves that facilitate this push. Rather, I ascertain that education and learning in general, leadership training and leaderships specifically, need an affective component to work and that experience surpasses knowledge. The affective components are those that involve the nonlinguistic ways in which entities (people, objects) include or take each other up in the world. I speak of a logic of intensities and the affective nature of language exchanges and political involvement forcing concepts open to yet-unknown territories of thought, matters and potentialities, and constant breaks with patterns, customs, traditions, structures, discourses, and habits. Affect is thus seen as an act of thinking embodied and embedded in the maximum intensity of experience, as "a power to affect itself, an affect of self on self" (Deleuze, 1988, p. 101), with affect theory ultimately reontologizing the real and arguing that sensations rather than knowledge might motivate action (read leadership).

Going via affect, the concept and impact of experience is put into play, opening up new individual, but also possible collective, learning trajectories. Or, put differently, the focus on affect radically changes how experiences are sensed, revealing how learning is transindividual and plugged into the environment. With reference to theories of learning, this implies an expansion of current dominating sociocultural learning theories, including affective aspects of language and learning in addition to cognitive and social aspects. I think we need new ways of working and leading, and expanded rationales for learning. In other words, to be involved in new forms of common intellectual practices, working and leading the work, that is, to trigger and help each other ask new questions always.

This chapter is therefore both a critique and rejection of a unitary vision of the subject as a self-regulating rationalist entity, and of a traditional image of thought and of the scientific knowledge practices that rest upon it. These are practices historically developed within the *linguistic turn*[1] of research and science and structured along axes of self-reflexive individualism and self-evident scientific rationality, indexed on a linear notion of time (Chronos) and a teleological[2] vision of the purpose of both scientific thought and human existence. Affect notions of time – and I add space – are embraced in a completely different manner, as Aion.[3] Time and space both become ambivalent about boundaries, so being a part of a time and a place means being in dynamic and nomadic relationships with both. The "time" represented by Chronos therefore can be said to be a keeper of institutional time divided into past, present, and future and, through this, the upholder of the authority of past discourses. The "time" represented by Aion is unbounded, dynamic, insurgent, and a more cyclical time of becoming, of flux. Building on Deleuze (1988), the continuity between the present and the actual, Chronos and Aion (via Kairos), activate multiple genealogical lines of resonance. Sameness and otherness coincide. Applied to competence building and knowledge creating practices, Chronos, generally speaking, tends to support mainstream, majority, and protocol-bound science/knowledge processes; "Aion, on the other hand, produces 'minor' ... science/ knowledge, which is, ..., ethically transformative and politically empowering. ... – is nomadic and defines the

---

[1] This is a huge debate, but generally speaking, it concerns the power, position, and function of language in and for meaning-making and change. As you will see, when we include affective aspects in language – affective language – the power, position, and function of language change.

[2] (In philosophy) the *belief* that everything has a *special purpose* or use; https://dictionary.cambridge .org/us/dictionary/english/teleology (retrieved October 29, 2020).

[3] The ancient Greeks had three conceptions time: *Chronos, Kairos, and Aion.* Chronos refers to chronological or sequential time. Kairos signifies a proper or opportune time for action, meaning the right, critical, or opportune moment. While Chronos is quantitative, Kairos has a qualitative, permanent nature. Aion (Greek: Αἰών) is a Hellenistic deity associated with time, the orb or circle encompassing the universe, and the zodiac. In the past, we had social and cultural mechanisms by which to bring Aion into Chronos, via Kairos, that is, to bring the sacred into the profane with the cultivated present. This is fundamentally the role that ritual (see note 6) plays, because in a proper ritual, people repeat a sacred cyclical action in the profane linear time, which, when the time is right, creates a bridge to the holy thing beyond our mundane experience.

research process as the creation of new concepts" (Braidotti, 2018, p. 17). I add learning and leadership *as* the creation of new concepts *as* change.

To be clear, this is a move away from leadership conceptualized within discourses and often divided into specializations of, for example, management, human resources, strategic, or pedagogical forms of leadership, to an integrated, holistic, and complex perspective of leadership in an educational connection. I wish to open up the leadership event and action itself toward new and multiple views on social and educational realities. I wish for increased attention to creativity and poetics, consciousness, and self-knowledge. I wish to contribute to increased mental mobility and learning, leadership for quality and innovation.

4.1   The Inseparability of Opposites

This is a sensorial and indirect approach to leadership, learning, change, and competence building informed by Gilles Deleuze and Félix Guattari's (2004a, b) transformational pragmatics. It is an approach for generating new possibilities, for both leadership and research on leadership, through attending to "less tangible" aspects of the politics of knowledge creation, leadership, and embodied and embedded learning. It implies adding value to "weak signals" in processes, hence taking into consideration both conscious and unconscious aspects of experience. It is a nondialectical politics of multiplicity ready to support and join a creative pluralism of educational organization. The inseparability of opposites, learning transmigrating throughout the aeons of time.

The concept of learning as embodied and embedded means that learning takes place in the whole body, within a person and between persons interacting in and with social and material realities. It includes gross motoric learning with visible movements, but also somatic movements taking place deep inside and between bodies. To put it short, I think that images, energy (force), and information or data are all we need in the development of new values and sensibilities around education and educational leadership, composing learning organizations. By turning to affect and to the affective side of working with concepts, leadership is pushed into a field where it is possible to ask what moves the different processes of learning and change, rather than what confirms or halts them. The concepts of leadership, organization, reading, writing, and affect are not just flipped but moved beyond the *known*. The same goes for the concepts of subject and object, problem and critique, de facto any concept. Ultimately, this secures children the right to a sensual childhood and agency, and professionals the paradoxical right and ability to subjective multiprofessional judgment.

4.2   Group-Decentered Anticipating Subjects with/in Writing Organizations

Elsewhere, and building on this, I argue that writing matters in leadership (Reinertsen, 2018; 2019; 2021; Reinertsen & Flatås, 2017; Thomas & Reinertsen, 2016). Further, that the type of leadership and leadership training that I advocate can also be seen as processes of being exposed to poetry, as being exposed to change. The poet is one "who lets loose molecular populations in hopes that this will sow the seeds of, or even engender, the people to come, that these populations will pass into a people to come, open a cosmos" (Deleuze & Guattari, 2004b, p. 381). The point is that there is a low threshold for inclusiveness, inclusive participation with thought that is, and the rightfulness of stakeholders through presence. Educational and poetic leaderships, or what I prefer to call edupoetic leaderships, through this become active minoritarian and responsive leaderships and/of inclusive designs through affective languages and writing. Writing seen as a virtual complex endeavor and, again, at best a way of leading and composing learning organizations and organizational learning. Bodies, minds, words, texts, habits, practices, images, sounds, pictures, experiences, etc. come together and talk back to one another. Emergent leaderships are produced through imperceptible tendencies and potentialities, the unavailable plasticity and immaterial aspects of formation. The sensory experience of change, culture, vulnerability, forgiveness, growth, learning, and unlearning are all interconnected and linked. Leadership, through this, is ultimately conceptualized change. And, to be clear, not the change of the individual subject, particular groups or systems, from one state to another; rather, change is seen as a "giving to the world the power to change us, to 'force' our thinking" (Stengers, 2008, p. 57).

I speak of group-decentered anticipating subjects with/in writing organizations. In Chapter 5, I present a case-assemblage of this type. Going via affect, the body and the writing come together to create a hypermodal sensational experience. Writing anticipation thus turns text – hence this chapter – into a virtual essay. Through this, the overarching contribution of this chapter and the next becomes pragmatic, political, and ethical, and concerns the constitution of subjectivity and transformative citizenships in intergenerational and intragenerational perspectives. I argue that more attention to leadership and more research on leadership must be directed into the cartographic, *ethological,* and *noological* mechanisms at work in plastic universes of reference which transform the virtual and transfigure the dynamics of affect. Ethology is understood here as the study of "the relation of speed and slowness, of the capacities for affecting and being affected that characterize each thing" (Deleuze, 1988, p. 125); noology, "which is distinct from ideology," (and) "is precisely the study of images of thought, and their historicity. In a sense, it could be said that all this has no importance, that thought has never had anything but laughable gravity. But that is all it requires: for us not to take it seriously" (Deleuze & Guattari, 2004b, p. 415). Both mechanisms fuel the image of an inclusive rhizomatic writing machine and design. Such leaderships and writing are therefore neither neutral nor innocent, rather, paradoxically, brutal.

4.3 Brutality

Rachel is an author and artist. She arranges writing workshops.

She has collected thousands of texts:

> I cry in the car after workshops because I am so exhausted from respecting them all. Much of my enthusiasm comes from that. It is a learning with/in joy and definitely narcissist. Or rather, it is hard work with texts and a physical bodily joy over the hard work of learning to respect all. What I do with their texts afterwards is wishing them well, that they will somehow cope. Honesty is what I think is universal here and what others can get or take from me. I try to be a vibrant human being. (Interview, August 11, 2016)

4.4 Ethology, or the Inseparable Ethical Task of Change in Education and/as Leadership

I therefore also consider the prevailing descriptions of educational realities and leadership issues found in contemporary research, policy, and practice incomplete and insufficient. This is – as is perhaps obvious by now – not simply because what appears as success from one perspective is problematic when viewed differently, whereas what appears as failure may actually reveal something that is of crucial importance. It is much more subtle and indirect, informal, and disturbing. Neither paradigms of *cultivation* nor *Bildung, culturation* nor *existential education* for competence building and leadership, will therefore suffice unless introduced as provisional. I write of a type of provision that builds in dynamics from the start through giving voice also to unconscious processes and affects and, through this, turning every paradigm and concept into constant rehearsals or activist playgrounds and/or writinggrounds (a term I invented) in which to sense the more and the other; of processes of becoming authentic selves while becoming other, developing new habit breaking modalities for accommodation of differences and learning. I plea for monistic[4] affirmative education, educational leadership policies and practises grounded on immanent intra- inter-connections and generative differences: a transversal composition of multiple assemblages of active minoritarian and responsive liminoid leaders, of inclusion. Education and leadership as emergent and seen as simultaneous nomadic processes of speeding up when standing still. Leadership *as* change.

In a sensorial and indirect approach to education and leadership training informed by Gilles Deleuze and Felix Guattaris' transformational pragmatics, as we shall see, *rhizomatic* writing, dynamics, nonlinearity and affective responses are built into its logics. The rhizome is originally a biological or botanical concept, a botanical rhizome that apprehends multiplicities. Deleuze and Guattari, however, developed it into a philosophical concept and *image of thought* to describe theory and research that allows for multiple, nonhierarchical entry and exit points in data representation and interpretation. They created, through this, an image of thought and a model of experiential informal learning built on the explication of subtle signs, images, aesthetic and/or artistic signs as potential sources of meanings. Writing thus consists in activating subjects (leaders) to enter into new affective transversal assemblages, to co-create alternative ethical forces and political codes – in other words, and as shown in Chapter 5, to compose a learning organization. It is a life and dwelling as writing as change; in *Pure Immanence* (Deleuze, 2005), it a model in which the subject is seen as a structure of affectivity.

Informal or indirect education and leadership training and experiential learning are therefore not a form of chaotic education and definitely not a form of anti-education of/or free will. It is an approach to education that seeks to get knowledge to work and/to produce constant importance for those involved. It is a view of learning as collective processes and collectivity with/in learning and implies a change of learning cultures that sweep away the deadening disjunctions paralyzing the adventure of experience. Ultimately,

---

[4] Monism is the view that reality is one unitary organic whole with no independent parts (www.merriam-webster.com).

it is a view of culture as spreading like the surface of a body of water, spreading toward available spaces or trickling downward toward new.

I therefore advocate a type of leadership producing thought provocations or collapse, ushering organizations toward experiences that more closely resemble the particular – but simultaneously universal – in intensive level and desire it operates, activating the inseparable ethical task as change in education and/as leadership, new norms of radical inclusive and collective differences, leaderships constantly in the making from virtualities, events, and singularities. This does not imply a lack of reality and realisms, only that something takes part in actualizing processes. Immanent knowledge practices for emergent leaderships in which rhizomatic writing are key to create movements in professional judgments (not) competences and competence building. Forwarding, through this, a new concept of *quality as force* in our daily practices, leadership for quality through movements actualized through problems as processual events. From this perspective, the object in work with leadership and competence building in theory and practice becomes work with processes of transcurricular *becomings and affect,* rather than, for example, different leadership programs predominantly mirroring a growing focus on management and the development of audit education cultures. And, to underline, "Affect is not, prescriptive. It is promissory. What it promises is intensity" (Massumi, 2015, p. 209).

4.5   Reontologizing the Real

This implies a move toward an *ontological* or *ontoepistemological turn*[5] in leadership and leadership studies, research, and science, expanding on what might matter in knowledge creation, meaning-making, learning, and change besides conscious conceptualization through language. Rather, leadership, research, and science conducted through a logics of intensities and thought of as emergent, embodied, and embedded processes of *time-space meaning mattering,* creating liminoid[6] moments of importance for

---

[5] The term ontoepistemological implies that ontology and epistemology cannot be separated. It is developed through the works among others of Jacques Derrida (1930–2004) albeit he spoke mainly of onto-ontologies, Gilles Deleuze (1925–1995) and Felix Guattari (1930–1992), and later Karen Barad (1956–) and Donna Haraway (1944–) to mention a few. The concepts of natureculture and theorypractice show the same inseparability as multiplicities.

[6] In the context of anthropology, the term liminoid describes the experience of the liminal stage of transience that occurs to the self during rituals as rites of passage. Here, the term is extended into the context of different types of biographical texts, ethnography and writing, liminalities as multiplicities (more below).

those concerned; engagement with imaginations of ourselves and others. The focus is the ongoing becomings that constantly transform the world (Deleuze & Guattari, 2004b) and change is ongoing in all aspects of life and learning. Guattari (2008) writes:

> While the logic of discursive sets endeavours to completely delimit its objects, the logic of intensities, or eco-logic, is concerned only with the movement and intensity of evolutive processes. Process, which I oppose to system or to structure, strives to capture existence in the very act of its constitution, definition and deterritorialization. This process of "fixing-into-being" relates only to expressive subsets that have broken out of their totalizing frame and have begun to work on their own account, overcoming their referential sets and manifesting themselves as their own existential indices, procedural lines of flights. (p. 30)

This calls into question the anthropomorphic logic framing ideas about agency, that is, willful (human) intentionality, and insisting that agencies are relational, co-constituted and constantly becoming through processes of intra-action. Rather, what I advocate is a science and practices showing that affect is a powerful component of – and condition for – leadership, learning, and hence organizational learning and possible change. Bearing connotations of bodily intensity, as a passion, as pathos, sympathy, and empathy, affect brings to the fore the anticipatory aspect and power of imagination; hence the secret in leadership and organizational learning lies in bringing thoughts into existence and not to judge. Instead, doing away with judgment and opening up friction zones between actual and virtual multiplicities that replace positioning, interests, linearity, and top-down control with enfoldedness, relations between bodies, and becomings, possibilizing and mobilizing interactionalist ontologies and/of viscous porosity.

In this way, leadership is seen as a constant grapple with relationally generated, hybrid, multilayered, often internally contradictory, interconnected and web-like agencies, and the need to attend to what this makes possible in attempts to extend figurations of leadership, learning, and change. Leadership is understood as a diffractive practice of contestation and creation through which new insights and practices can e/merge. These emergent leaderships maintain focus on procedurality itself as it is, and on how to keep processes open to avoid closing knowledge creation down and turning to management by objectives too quickly. By broadening and transforming notions of leadership and learning, I therefore want to contribute to moving away from measuring effects in skills, knowledge, and competence, toward an expanded focus on affective aspects for leadership for knowledge sharing and learning in organizations; increase our vocabularies for sensed practices; increase and expand on our endurance and limits of tolerance toward difference and different expressions. This, in turn, is a contribution to the child grounded in inclusive humanisms.

It is the concept and notion of the virtual, hence writing as a virtual endeavor, that leads us toward what I call a *rhizomatic – as a poetic schizoanalytical –* writing machine. Writing as simultaneous method and means for education and learning, leaders, and leaderships. The writing leader develops conceptual foci while also, and at the same time, designing for debate. Affective language and/as writing ultimately becomes a condition for learning and collaboration in organizations – organizational learning.

A rhizome breaks all patterns and creates anew, as lines and points, which affectively collapse with/in themselves, and is like a constant ethological and noological writing – or machinic short-term memory – creating constant new movements and dynamic maps for leadership and learning, educative quality in/of organizations. Creating, with this, shifting subject positions within quantum flows of processing information and/or what I have chosen to call *dataphilosophy* (Reinertsen, 2020). Dataphilosophy involves explorations of what leadership actually encompasses through critique of a flattened and linear rationale and assumption of neutral knowledge creation and teleological competence building. Instead, it argues that leadership and consequently perceived subjectivities – knowledge and quality – are much more interconnected and complex. Through this, a critical stance is taken against the mesmerising modes of representation that run rampant across our ocular territories.

4.6 Moving beyond the Known

This chapter and Chapter 5, are, as I have indicated, also a critique of what it means to be knowledgeable and know something, ultimately what competence and competence building *as* leaders and *for* leaderships might imply. Both chapters offer a view of emergent leaderships produced through the imperceptible tendencies and potentialities, the unavailable plasticity and immaterial aspects, of worlding formation. Embodied and embedded processes are viewed as simultaneously immanent, relational, affective, and situated. Worlding is seen as relations between percepts, affects, and concepts leading to novel concepts in/for experience. These are immanent postpositivist knowledge practices of bringing simultaneously to the fore disqualified knowledges through which criticism performs its work and with it a return of knowledge; constant processes of creating something new with what empirically *is* through situating oneself in the middle and moving (it) closer. It puts the concept of agency in play as *agencement*[7] and vital for opening up spaces for writing and change, hence – and again, indirectly – both the anticipatory spaces and power of imagination. Deleuze and Guattari treat agents as collective subjects of ongoing events, meaning that agents never act in the first person, but rather as a "collectively immanent third-person" (Deleuze & Guattari, 1994, pp. 64–65) of a case-assemblage. Manning (2019) states that "agencement . . . draws the event into itself. It is a forward force capable of carrying the affective tonality of non-conscious resonance and mowing it toward the articulation, edging into consciousness, of new modes of existence."

I sometimes speak of the *placebo effect* of learning and leadership. The concept of placebo refers to inactive treatment that nevertheless gives positive physiological, behavioral, emotional, and cognitive effects on the person who is involved. It is the result of positive expectations and says something about the potential of exploiting one's own potential and own strengths for learning. The concept of critique is turned into an expression of engagement for inclusion, and immanence is seen as trans- and/or *incorporeal* (Grosz, 2017) moments of evaluation of experience when a subject cedes her place to a life. Life forces are pursuing its tendencies, and every moment or flash is seen to be carrying its future. In *aeon*, presence evaporates and becomes a part of past and future simultaneously. Again, Deleuze and Guattari (2004b) write "Aeon: the indefinite time of the event, the floating line that knows only speeds and continually divides that which transpires into an already-there that is at the same time not-yet-there, a simultaneous too-late and too-early" (p. 289).

Here is an illustration. I have moved it to the other side of the page for joy.

Quotes from Focus Group Interview with Kindergarten Leaders February 25, 2020[8]

LEADER: You know, I have attended different classes (courses) . . . on one
                  occasion, I sat there and learned a sentence together with two other
                  colleagues, and I know that one of them changed 100% in her meetings

---

[7] The French word *agencement* translates narrowly to English as "arrangement," "fitting," or "fixing." The Deleuze and Guattarian term "assemblage" originally stems from *agencement*. "*Agencement* asserts the inherent implication of the connection between specific concepts and that the arrangement of those concepts is what provides sense or meaning. Assemblage, on the other hand, can be more accurately described as the integration and connection of these concepts and that it is both the connections *and* the arrangements of those connections that provide context for assigned meanings" (https://sosiologen.no [retrieved June 2, 2022]; my translation).

[8] Part of my rule-breaking grammar and languaging is genre and text mixing. In addition, I move texts toward the other side of the page to break them up. I hope that I make you stop and ask why. Maybe it irritates you a bit? As a leader you might want to ask yourself what your language and how you use concepts does for the people you lead and how to create more and other together? Problem as force . . .

with children after this <u>one</u> sentence in that class. In this way, I guess one could have measured something, but I guess that makes it rather random ...

INTERVIEWER: Measure what? The competences of the grown up who changes his/her practice and that this brings something good to or for the children?

LEADER: That ... is the difficult ... How to measure that? It is like when we are asked to measure inclusiveness. How do I measure that?

INTERVIEWER: My suggestion is don't.

> World instead.
> Produce unconscious.
> Be intuitive and try to put yourself – read and write – in a poetic mode.
> Place yourself in the world as if that is the meaning of life itself and drift along.
> Every step you take remains in you body as a map in which you yourself
>   is the scale,
> with consistencies and smells, colors and noises,
> and the patterns that are formed
> gradually embrace more and more of the world.
> Leaderships spoken by life.
> Is problem, is force is data.

Deleuze writes (2002b):

> Producing unconscious has thus nothing to do with e.g. reproduction of childhood memories or any repressed memories or phantasms, but has all to do with non-personal powers producing "blocs of childhood" which are always in the present. We produce not with a core from which we emerge, nor with the people who attach us to it, nor with images that we draw from it, nor with any structures of development or growth. We produce – "with the scrap of placenta which we have hidden, and which is always contemporary with us, as raw material to experiment with." (p. 78)

4.7   The Image of an Inclusive Rhizomatic Writing Machine and Design

> In reality *writing does not have its end in itself, precisely because life is not something personal.* Or rather, the aim of writing is to carry life to the state of a non-personal power. (Deleuze, 2002c, p. 50; italics in original)

Here Deleuze implies that, instead of working with concepts as a quest for definitions, we should work to keep concepts open for something unexpected, something we have not thought about before, as a move from the constative to the unknown. The unknown, however, through affect, is simultaneously very close, a gut feeling perhaps, and/as a "dynamic 'evaluation' that is lived out in the situation" (Massumi, 2010, p. 338). Every moment or event through this becomes a moment of liminality and is seen as activist processes, not of assessment but of evaluation of experience. This means liminalities are not simply a rite of passage, but something that crosses timespaces and can be a site of awareness, silence, and resistance within the contemporary moment. Liminalities are seen through this as multiplicities of ontological positions that ultimately challenge entrenched modes of leadership and are *twisted* (Carlson et al., 2020; Reinertsen, 2020), making possible the realization of more-than-human concepts such as the disintegration of subjectivity: subjectobject, natureculture, and theorypractice liminalities as "asignifying and asubjective multiplicities" (Deleuze & Guattari, 2004b, p. 10*).* Further, that such multiplicities are "designated by indefinite articles, or rather by partitives (... *some* of a rhizome ...)" (2004b, p. 10; italics in original). Deleuze and Guattari (1994) write:

> There are no simple concepts ... There is no concept with only one component ... Every concept is at least double or triple, etc. ... In a concept, there are parts or components of other concepts ... Concepts are centres of vibrations, each in itself and everyone in relation to all others. (pp. 15–23)

And, "A new rhizome may form in the heart of a tree, the hollow of a root, the crook of a branch. Or else it is a microscopic element of the root-tree, a radicle, that gets rhizome production going" (Deleuze & Guattari, 2004b, p. 16). And, "Write, form a rhizome, increase your territory by deterritorialization, extend the line of flights to the point where it becomes an abstract machine covering the entire plane of consistency" (Deleuze & Guattari, 2004b, p. 12).

A rhizome (see Figure 4.1) is therefore a force of nature and the possibilities of culture simultaneously, interdependent and interconditioned. The rhizome presents nature and culture as *natureculture* and as a map, or wide array, of attractions and influences with no specific origin or genesis. It is characterized *by* "ceaselessly established connections between semiotic chains, organizations of power, and circumstances relative to the arts, sciences, and social struggles" (Deleuze & Guattari, 2004b, p. 8). It stretches from chemical, physical, and biological cell and microscopic levels of particles to our abstract dreams and thoughts about, and in, life. "It has no beginning or end; it is always in the middle, between things,

Figure 4.1 Photograph of a rhizome.

interbeing, *intermezzo.* . . . the rhizome is alliance, uniquely alliance"
(Deleuze & Guattari, p. 27; italics in original). The planar movement of
the rhizome therefore resists chronology and organization; instead, it favors
a pragmatic or nomadic system and method of change, growth, and
propagation. It is real and virtual and "operates through variation, expansion, conquest, capture, offshoots" (2004b, p. 23). Elsewhere (Reinertsen,
2022) I have called this *the Art of Not Knowing and the Position of Non-
Knowledge as Activisms.* As such, the rhizome becomes an image, model,
and notion of the meaning of connections and movements and, again,
productions of constant importance of – and for – each/other. The
importance ultimately of – and for – the child.

> The nomad knows how to wait, he has infinite patience. Immobility and
> speed, catatonia and rush, a "stationary process", station as process . . . It is

thus necessary to make a distinction between *speed and movement*. A movement might be very fast, but that does not give it speed; a speed may be very slow, or even immobile, yet it is still speed. Movement is extensive; speed is intensive. Movement designates the relative character of a body considered as "one", and which goes from point to point; *speed, on the contrary, constitutes the absolute character of a body whose irreducible parts (atoms) occupy or fill a smooth space in a manner of a vortex, with the possibility of springing up at any point.* (Deleuze & Guattari, 2004b, p. 420; italics in original)

4.8   Minor Leadership and Research on Leadership

With reference to less tangible and *weak signals* within learning, this approach to leadership and learning implies acceptance of immanence, hence immanent microscopic or minor things or atoms in tiny perceptions, interpretations, dispositions, or inclinations, which simultaneously destabilize the same perceptions, interpretations, dispositions, or inclinations. Every object or subject, organic or not organic, has its own life and can only be experienced through tensions in its own moral mass and molecular parts. In this way, the rhizome becomes the image – as both method and means – of a leadership-writing machine as a constant creative reimagining of leadership; what leadership might produce. Constant new images of transitions and variations between, and of, subjects and objects of leadership. An ethic, a morale or moral action – here here of leadership – exists therefore only in matter in situ here and now and as minor, not major, processes. The now is comprised of masses of elements collapsing together and related to each other in expanded inter-intrarelational connections. I will come back to this when I expand on processes of constitution of subjectivity, but for now I confirm that, rather than dealing with subjects and objects, Deleuze (1993), through the rhizome, deals with objects as *objectiles* and subjects as *superjects*. Building on Whitehead (1938; [1920] 2015) and Simondon ([1958, 2012] 2017), Deleuze (1993) states that: "Just as the object becomes objectile, the subject becomes a superject" (p. 21). Subjectivities therefore dissolve and identity becomes a collectivity in which I/we de facto create my/our own data (read empiricism) collectively. Or, put differently, these are processes of collective individuation in a collectivity and a doing away with judgment. My/our rhizomatic becomes an event in which we together engage each other. Braidotti (2018) writes, "The nomadic lines of flight of minor sciences cut across, re-territorialize and re-compose the dominant knowledge production systems precisely through creating multiple missing links, opening generative cracks and inhabiting liminal spaces" (p. 19)

It is fruitful to take a closer look at the way Deleuze (1993) uses the concepts of "molecular" and "molar" to create a notion about connections between knowledge and materiality. They are both adjectives used within the subject area of chemistry, in which molecular refers to collections of molecules and molar refers to mass. A molecule further consists of two or more atoms forming a unity. As mentioned in Section 4.7, and with specific reference to the originally biological concept of the rhizome, Deleuze expands on concepts' application fields. As the rhizome is turned into a rhizomatic writing machine, writing as imagination, dataphilosophizing, and becomings, molecularity becomes related to decentered and individuated responses to phenomena or types of conducts in which the molecular is related to constant processes of/and recreation, or what can be called inter-intramolecular action. Further, the molar is also conceptualized as organs' and organisms' general patterns of conduct, and in the seminal work of *A Thousand Plateaus,* Deleuze and Guattari (2004b) apply both concepts on *political bodies* and, in this way, become capable of studying matter/materiality as a function of folds of fluidity, mass and hardness, *consistency and disintegration.* And, again, through this the political life and the study of life being about the now.

The understanding of a person, however, is not distinct and atomistic but is made up of the connections and relationships that people form as they interact and create knowledge together, or rather as they possibilize and mobilize space, arranging elements to create connections that are more likely to produce new knowledge or experiences. These are simultaneous processes concerned with how knowledge is formed and shared, social and inter-intrapersonal harmony, ensuring that peoples' knowledges and experience can be put to good use. The *writing organization* concept (Reinertsen, 2014; Thomas and Reinertsen, 2016) is a reflection of such processes as an inclusive design principal.

> A concept is a heterogenesis – that is to say, an ordering of its components by zones of neighbourhood. It is ordinal, an intention present in all the features that make it up. The concept is in a state of *survey (fr: survol)* in relation to its components, endlessly traversing them according to an order without distance. It is immediately co-present to all its components of variations, at no distance from them, passing back and forth through them: it is a refrain, an opus with its number *(fr: chiffre)*. (Deleuze & Guattari, 1994, p. 21)

4.9   Edupoetics; Forcing Our Thinking; Letting go of Judgment

Theorizing further, edupoetics[9] is a direction in educational philosophy and research emphasizing the role of imagination and poetry, signs, linguistic, and material alike, in human experience and the included – as opposed to excluded – middles. The writing leader creates inclusive debate designed for opening up for moments of awareness and calmness. Inclusive design is thus thought of as a move and extension of a set of knowledges and rights located in the abstract future in relation to political struggles that are integral to learning: the right to rewrite and/or reauthor knowledges and rights. Further, and through the politics of the moment, knowledgeable rightfulness is established through presence: making visible the intersections of knowledges and justice/injustice in the present while being oriented toward new educational and social futures. The burden or cost of inclusion is shared between learners and a culture of hospitality; an ethical commitment to leverage guest–host relationships is replaced by a culture of disruption toward knowledges and justice, where modes of power/authority are collectively called into question toward coconstructive equitable ends. In life as in research, the problem arises not in bodies themselves, but in the troubles that bodies meet. Thus, this is ultimately a perspective and attempt to explore forms of leadership that might create a more distinct culture for exploration and sharing. It is an educational philosophy, hence building in foresight in/as research and imagining the making of educational futures. Edupoetics does not therefore limit itself to the analysis of formal education and leadership issues, but addresses informal pedagogies in practice, in life, and embodied and embedded knowledges. (I am in good company; John Dewey [1859–1952] throughout his oeuvre explicitly denies the possibility to educate directly.)

Edupoetics implies focusing on the unconscious in thought as much as the unknown in the body or moving thinking from its position within the conscious toward the unconscious or unknown in thought and the unconscious or unknown in the body. The aim is not to create any new subjects or objects, educational or leadership models or programs, to see the unconscious, or to create meanings from the unconscious, but to produce the unconscious to open up for multiple new thoughts and always other

---

[9] See also the term *exopedagogy* (Semetsky, 2020, p. 2). It indicates an alternative form of education that exceeds a solely human dimension. It represents a form of posthumanist education. It is a radical form of cultural, experiential, and postformal pedagogy. It transgresses the boundaries of narrow rationality and takes education out of its habitual bounds. Exopedagogy is "located" in culture, in experience, and in life.

desires. It turns leadership into, or to become conceptualized as, a pulse for action and for sensing attention, formation, and values, not just educability and duties. Leaders/poets who think and act with/in every possibility within every situation. Leaders/poets who perform leadership with events and activities, not individuals. Leaders/poets who lead through emergent experimentations and generative curiosity. And, with reference to the concept of problem again: leaders/poets who therefore never try to avoid any problem. Rather, leaders/poets who create problems by producing tensions, which propel or trigger thoughts for constant innovation. Any problem is turned into an epistemic force and/as thinking-possibility only and experiential judgment is "critical and clinical" (Deleuze, 1989). Any problem is seen as a bringing "into existence and not to judge" (p. 135)[10] an opportunity to create interruptions or absences that allow difference to be reconciled. Valuing the necessity of difference, difference that can enable collaboration and connectedness. Deleuze continues:

> What expert judgment, in art, could ever bear on the work to come? It is not a question of judging other existing beings, but of sensing whether they agree or disagree with us, that is, whether they bring forces to us, or whether they return us to the miseries of war, to the poverty of the dream, to the rigors of organization. As Spinoza had said, it is a problem of love and hate and not judgment; "my soul and body are one ... What my soul loves, I love. What my soul hates, I hate ... All the subtle sympathizing of the incalculable soul, from the bitterest hate to passionate love." This is not subjectivism, since to pose the problem in terms of force, and not in other terms, already surpasses all subjectivity. (p. 135)

To elaborate further on affect, affective language and moments being the only bearing structure of communication and knowledge creation, is about language again: Drawing from Baruch de Spinosa's (1632–1677) affectus, *l'affect* is an ability to affect and be affected. It is "a prepersonal intensity corresponding to the passage from one experiential state of the body to another and implying an augmentation or diminution in that body's capacity to act" (Massumi, 1987, p. xvi). Through this, affect is an intensity, *something/it* that goes through my body without necessarily leading to any specific meaning, but makes me responsive, vulnerable perhaps, but in a productive way. It is something that is affecting me/us beyond emotions and beliefs hence beyond factual power struggles over

[10] Deleuze builds on the work of Baruch de Spinoza (1632–1677) who spoke of *Amor intellectualis Dei* as love of God, love of knowledge, love of thinking and freedom through an ethics of Joy.

authority. Rather, it is something that is urging me to proceed by inquiry, and my attention and readiness is directed toward that which emerges and in turn contributes to un/consciousness about the situated meaning and value of knowledge. It possibilizes an activist production of importance of knowledge sensed there and then, with molecular vibrations however as the only truth. Massumi (2002) writes:

> When you affect something, you are at the same time opening yourself up to being affected in turn, and in a slightly different way than you might have been the moment before. Affect is therefore, a threshold experience, or in my *words*, an *affective entrance* where a **transition** becomes possible in everyday life which is necessarily **(em)bodied** (p. 41; bold text and italics in original).

Every act of language involves an expression of affect. Affect is thus seen as *infra* conditioning every determinate activity, including that of language. Again, Massumi (2015) writes:

> The preferred prefix for affect is "infra-". The prefix of "pre" connotes time sequence, but affect always accompanies, on the parallel track of potential. "Intra-" is also imprecise, connoting as it does space and containment (from interus, internal). "Infra-" on the other hand connotes what actively lies below a certain threshold of appearance on an open-ended spectrum (as in "infrared"; from inferus). (p. 212)

Affect and language are therefore not opposites: "There is no antinomy between affect and language. There is accompaniment and becoming, always involving the full spectrum of the graded continuum of experience" (Massumi, 2015, p. 212). Affect and language are infra connected and infra dependent. Leaders and staff through this become "a motif for each other, both embedded in a transcoded passage" (Semetsky, 2013, p. 229) going through a "shared deterritorialization" (Deleuze & Guattari, 2004b, p. 324); an immanent creative production of group decentered subjectivities and rhizomatic writing.

The creative in leadership can be recognized in productive connection between creative practice and thinking practice: leading as/through thinking and thinking as/through leading. Creativity is, through this, seen as a fundamentally methodological quality. The methodologicity involved is emphatically experimental and comfortable with knowledge production in uncertainty, multiplicity, and friction. Thinking with, through, and beyond concepts, creative leaders become creative in designing and developing their own methods and approaches, as they seek to navigate and explore the productive connections and reciprocal relationships between the creative practices they engage with, and to develop conceptual analytical approaches for what these practices also work with, through, or beyond. I am tempted to say that these are evidence producing leaders and organizations again and again – but not, since no evidence lasts for ever.

4.10 Constitution of Leadership Subjectivities

Attention to constitutions of subjectivity in general, and leadership subjectivities in particular, knowledge creation, and competence building, are therefore vital. Attention to, and engagements in, conversations with the myriad complexities that arise from seeing subjectivity as becoming(s); the ability to navigate shifting knowledge landscapes within the potential of collective subjectivities, human and nonhuman. This is to get away from postpositivist thinking and unbridled optimisms of connections in organizations, in learning, and in science and research alike. Further, situating rich and complex views of leaderships in the making that eschew simplistic notions of *equity*, *quality* or *access* to particular forms of educational provision and models. Deleuze (1993) writes:

> The life of the individual has given way to an impersonal and yet singular life, which foregrounds a pure event that has been liberated from the accidents of internal and external life, that is, from the subjectivity and the objectivity of what comes to pass: a «homo tantum» with whom everyone sympathizes and who attains a kind of beatitude; or an ecceity, which is no longer an individuation, but a singularization, a life of pure immanence, neutral, beyond good and evil, since only the subject that incarnated it in the midst of things made it good or bad. The life of such an individuality is eclipsed (s'efface au profit) by the singular immanent life of a man who no longer has a name, though he can be mistaken for no other. A singular essence, a life . . . .. (pp. 386–387)

To elaborate, a liminoid experience defines an undetermined set of rules that triggers a transformation in the sense of self. A/The leader does not therefore simply translate mental processes directly, but engages participants in the mental process and, through this, the leader opens a term or concept up and possibilizes an extended meaning. The liminoid in organizations are, in fact, the participants, who become somewhat like liminal androids, elusive organisms that become pure form for the transition from one identity to the other. The virtual space of/in organization offers an endless multitude of forms and folds, it appears both everywhere and nowhere at the same time, and thus this space is inherently liminoid.

The virtual space is the ideal place to experience the modes of appearance and disappearance of the idea of the self. In contrast to what occurs within everyday experience, there is no fixed position for the sense of self. It is thus in constant becoming, conditioned by the entirety of the human experience, both physical and mental. The folding and unfolding of subjectivity are represented by machinic or concentric shapes. The constant fluid folding, unfolding, and dispersion of concepts and texts are an aesthetic representation of our temporal and spatial configurations, which produce new modes of subjectivity. The point of (dis)orientation becomes a deep, dark dimension that allows us to lose and recuperate ourselves. The liminoid as an interface for human liminoid experience is a product of poetically generated images and sounds, but at the end of the day, the effects depend on our personal notions of timespace.

Hence, this is an attempt also to eschew the subject–object, nature–culture, time–space, theory–practice, body–mind/mind–matter, real–virtual, and individual–collective divides, to eschew "any conception of the mind or ideality and body, or materiality, as separate substances – in order to develop a nonreductive monism or a paradoxical dualist monism" (Grosz, 2017, p. 249). Rather it is an attempt to create transitions between subjects and objects, between nouns and verbs, between substances and processes; to create variations in objects that turn the object to an *objectile* (Simondon [1958, 2012] 2017) so that the object becomes an event that impacts the subject. Monism, thought of as unity of the origin of all things and all substances, involves thinking ideality and materiality together. It repeals nature–culture divides and allows explorations, experimentations and fabulations, movements, intensities, and potentialities. Focusing on sensations and intensities, provocations can produce meaning from something, an object, a piece of information or data, potentializing affective ECE leadership models. Affective moments of connectivities hence possibilize molecular becomings, minded-mattered languaging and inter-intrafactual practises and consilience[11] in leadership and learning, learning in organizations, and learning organizations. While languaging refers to the use and materiality of languages, consilience is about bringing forth new knowledge, here transcorporeal collectivities and transdisciplinary thinking. It is a monistic ontology that assumes radical immanence, that is, the primacy of intelligent and self-organizing matter implying "that the

---

[11] The linking together of principles from different disciplines especially when forming a comprehensive theory www.merriam-webster.com/dictionary/consilience (retrieved August 6, 2020).

posthuman knowing subject has to be understood as a relational embodied and embedded, affective and accountable entity and not only as a transcendental consciousness" (Braidotti, 2018, p. 1). Building on this, education and leadership training and competence building is seen as bringing the concepts of objectivity, subjectivity, knowledge, and competence – indeed, ultimately all concepts – into play and seeking to continue keeping them in play, or as we shall see, keeping them in writing or rather keeping them writing. "Concepts are only created as a function of problems which are thought to be badly understood or badly posed" (Deleuze & Guattari, 1994, p. 16). Consequently, all concepts are seen as critical concepts, as simultaneously methodological and performative. And with reference to both the concepts of critique and information and/or data:

> [Critique] concerns the tendencies that the introduction of the facto actively brings into the situation. It is the actual, eventful consequences of how the factors plays out, relationally with any number of other factors that also activate tendentially, and in a way that is utterly singular, specific to those situated co-expressions (Massumi, 2010 p. 338)

This is why Deleuze (1998) speaks of critique as a *clinical practice*: as the diagnostic art of following the dynamic signs of constant unfoldings, which can then be actively modulated from within the situation, immanent to it. The *knowing* subject (read leader) is hence seen as "multiplicity, process and becoming" (Braidotti, 2010, p. 211). It represents a decentered subject with/in multiple and multimodal voices, pluri voiced and voices in the plural. It is a subject open to flux and holder of a *zetetic*[12] curiosity constantly expanding the inquiring mind. It is a becoming *with* that which emerges, movements of qualitative change, continual variations, tiny intersections, *minor gestures* (Manning, 2019) on experience. Consequently, leaderships and research on leaderships are turned into a living and writing forward understanding backward; knowledge creation with/in the affective language of care, critique, and collective responsibility for learning, hence learning organizations – languages that write, writing languages, *proceduralized* language and languaging.

And to elaborate even further, this implies a move beyond the mere critique of both the identitarian category of a sovereign self and dominant subject position on the one hand and the image of thought that equates

---

[12] Zetesis, or in ancient Greek ζήτησις, means search, examination, or inquiry www.merriam-webster .com (retrieved March 4, 2020).

subjectivity with rational consciousness and learning on the other. Rather, this is about learning *with* the unconscious, the unconscious of thought – as the yet-unthought-of – at the cognitive level. The unconscious (of the mind) is considered to be just as profound as the unknown in the body, at the level of affects and encounters, generating knowledge but never conceptualized as fixed. Even as a concept inhabits our experience in its as yet unconscious or virtual form, the ethical task remains. The ethical task "to set up . . . to extract" (Deleuze & Guattari, 1994, p. 160) the very "sense" of this empirical event as the newly created concept in our "actual" practice (Semetsky, 2020, p. 6). It is a constant realization of concepts or languaging as writing as plugging back in or putting the X/radical back in empiricism. Deleuze (1994) writes:

> The plurivocity of the concept depends solely upon neighbourhood (one concept can have several neighbourhoods). Concepts are flat surfaces without levels, orderings without hierarchy; hence the importance in philosophy of the questions "What to put in a concept?" and "What to put with it?" What concept should be put alongside a former concept, and what components should be put in each? These are the questions of the creation of concepts. (p. 90)

4.11 The Schizoanalytical Writingground of/for Leadership

Leadership *as* change *as* a rhizomatic writing machine becomes a commitment to reinvention and infinite variation, to follow the paths of individual vicissitudes and the sufferings and joys of the worlds in which we live, and to courageously imagine better futures, better and learning organizations. "A method of the rhizome type, . . . can analyse language only by decentering it onto other dimensions and other registers. A language is never closed upon itself, except as a function of impotence" (Deleuze & Guattari, 2004b, p. 8). The rhizome and the awareness of the preliminary nature of knowledge creates processes across preliminary borders, opens up for translations and interpretations outside of known vocabularies and through unfinished channels. Rhizomatic writing becomes attractive as a condition to position oneself in an imperceptible but urgent affect, which can evolve into a strong force of energy for change, developing new values and sensibilities around education and educational leadership.

I have stressed that concepts are not just flipped, but moved beyond the *known*. This is important to bear in mind to avoid taken-for-granted expectations of stakeholders writing complete stories or stringent narratives within organizations and learning. Process must be deauthorized and low-threshold, inclusive of different expressions. A single word might sometimes be enough. Sentences, examples, or cases might appear abrupt and incomplete. That is OK. One might challenge grammatical rules and invent new words. One might play with styles and genres. Such messy writing is productive, deliberate even, and part of a plea for constant openness and innovation in organization, escaping the legacy of the linguistic turn in which conceptualization and definitions, sadly but often, are mistaken as truths. Affective languages and writing, on the other hand, turn any truth and any concept into a work in progress and truthfulness is what we work and hope for. And, to be crystal clear, objectivity is the ultimate goal but will here only "assume a certainty of knowledge rather than presuppose a truth recognized as pre-existing, or already there" (Deleuze & Guattari, 1994, p. 27). Sometimes this proves brutal and in the early childhood facility that I have worked with, we sometimes cried.

As you have seen in Section 4.4, I invent the term *writingground*. A writingground for leadership, learning, and change, leadership and learning *as* change, learning organizations. This then, is my virtual and dynamic writingground and essay. Through writing, I become my own work in progress and meta-meta perspective of my own writing. Therefore, I invite you also to write (read virtually), *intuitively* or *affectively* and come as you are. The fact is that Deleuze and Guattari's pragmatics is difficult and this chapter on leadership with such pragmatics is also somewhat difficult. Through intuitive reading and writing, however, one does not have to follow every proposition, make every connection. The intuitive or affective reading may therefore even be more practical and again – poetic. Hurley, when translating Deleuze's (1988) text from French into English asks: "What if one accepted the invitation – come as you are – and read with a different attitude, which might be more like the way one attends to poetry? Then difficulty would not prevent the flashes of understanding that we anticipate in the poets we love, difficult though they may be" (p. iii). Here, such flashes can be thought of as this *humorous – short-term-memory – ethological and noological writing machine* in which minds might shift their place. The moment being the only bearing structure communicating something/X, hence what we anticipate, and knowledge creation. All in all, this is an *edupoetic* and indirect attempt to bring the child more clearly into leadership issues. It is a *schizoanalytical* – becoming child – becoming leader – formation or modeling, forcing my thinking, hence what I must. Deleuze and Guattari (2004a) write:

> The task of schizoanalysis is ... to reach the investments of unconscious desire of the social field, insofar as they are differentiated from the preconscious investments of interest, and insofar as are not merely capable of counteracting them, but also of coexisting with them in opposite modes. (p. 383)

4.12   Case-Assemblage Onward

As a simultaneous summing up and forwarding to Chapter 5: we live in a paradoxical knowledge situation, in society and in institutions or organizations alike. Increasing amounts of factual knowledge produce lack of clarity, for some a felt inflated chaos, loss of value, and therefore loss of impact. It is a condition experienced by some as a loss of power of definition, as power knowledge fights for factual authority. Therefore, it is for some a negative condition and a condition seemingly demanding corrections, often conceptualized as actions, efforts, and use of energy to come back to something that used to be, or forward to something better than before. Results from such thinking can be seen in different degrees and strengths of increased polarization and subsequent uniformity, increased micromanagement, and institutionalized instrumentalism; even worse, in powerlessness, loss of trust, and various degrees of institutionalized cynicism. This way, and in a power knowledge perspective, knowledge might in itself appear as something negative, sometimes almost dangerous, something that we must be either for or against; some knowledges and someone's knowledges seen as either good or bad, consequently some policies and leaderships thought to be value based, others not. These are oversimplifications and misconceptualizations, which might have unwanted and unforeseen consequences, such as connections between subjectivity, knowledge, and learning possibly being experienced as incomprehensible and dysfunctional.

Thus, the more important rethinking education and learning, leadership, and research on leadership becomes. Thinking anew about the development of leaders and the purposes of their work as immanent practices of critique and about the critic/leader as a poet trying to reach beyond the work that she considers. Ultimately, her body is/as profession. Chapter 5 is an example and *case-assemblage* (Andersson et al. 2020) of leadership and a writing organization. What happens in the machinery of a case-assemblage is that things are *felt, desired, and produced* (Andersson et al. 2020). And as should be overly clear by now, such case-assemblages are more than mixtures of diverse factors and elements. They entail constructive processes that lay out multiple creative characteristics that organize and "define" their arrangement. They consist of various relations within which concrete elements and productions appear and become visible in the moment; various concrete elements meet each other and one element creates a flow, which is broken by another element. They support combinations of concrete elements and admit the possibility of their simultaneous occurrences. The agents – or or rather -agents – in case-assemblages are nomadic figures able to write and rewrite various elements together according to their virtual relations. And to be clear, this is not about learning from a traditional case study and best practice. Therefore, it is vital to continue to read intuitively to get concepts and knowledges to work; concepts willing to work together with matters and matters willing to work together with concepts. Thinking about learning, thinking, knowing, and leading in the making: messiness becoming a resource in our efforts and aspirations.

Leaderships through knowing life, learning life, learning life together, and then what leaders and leadership produce. Leadership about learning difference. Patience and willingness to sacrifice the required time. Leadership and leaders carrying the hardships but liberated from it. Leadership and leaders living in a place of pictures, sounds, smells, humans, sorrows, joys, phenomena, trips, and landscapes, strange and funny, in a fine-grained web of thoughts.

CHAPTER 5

Knowledge Possibilizing
A Transgressional Learning and Leadership Model

Anne

> I want every employee to feel safe and simultaneously sense a need to excel in his or her position and role. Life in kindergarten is complex, and consists to a substantial degree of making choices according to what every employee must prioritize in every relation throughout the everyday work. It requires every one of us to develop flexible practices. Decisions must be made and made again and again. (Micronarrative of nursery general manager, 2017)

This chapter and case-assemblage on leadership challenges a conventional conception of what a case study might be. It is not a still picture or example conditioned by certain criteria and frozen in time, but a dynamic and productive case-assemblage produced through the affective nature of language and every concept contains zones of friction or swirling organizations constantly expanding on specific, different, and transformable nuances of leadership and knowledge renewing. It implies, as we have seen in Chapter 4, a radical shift that theorizes the production of leadership as impersonal affective flows that produce various capacities in exploring bodies; intensities rather than intentions become the focus of attention.

When orienting toward affective nuances in leadership and learning organizations, the order of authorities is disturbed. Relations are under co-composition, and every stakeholder makes an impact. Affect, there among intensities, moves across processes of learning and collaboration, and mobilizes a quality of the relations. It is complex, paradoxical, and never ending. The inseparability of opposites produces the positive as the absence of negative, the right as the absence of wrong. Every subject and object, every moment of liminoid nothingness, every I and collective we, containing multitudes.

In writing and writing organizations, hence case-assemblages, there are exterior multiplicities of conscious ordering, measuring, differentiating, and extensiveness associated with predetermined knowledges. There are interior multiplicities of unconscious, intensive, libidinal, and impulsive evolvements associated with novelty. And again, this implies processes of conceptualization as thinking and doing of both positive and negative, right and wrong at the same time. Innovation and change are thus seen as open-ended processes of constantly intensifying something without directing it to a certain place or center. Rather, frictions continue where the actualization of the virtual and the virtualization of the actual are going on.

As far as judgment is concerned, and unlike external judgments acting upon us with influences from the outside, such simultaneous assessments are interior, and productions of affects are at work in our relations. This unpredictable change is therefore a multiplicity of virtual organization, relational, unconscious, and irrevocably experienced, rather than predetermined, conscious, and measurable. Intensity and excitement in leadership and learning imply therefore deep experience, of both relationality and practice, leadership established through presence, and always politicized.

Going beyond representation, a case-assemblage is not a best practice to try to copy, only an example of processes from which to draw inspiration and, in that respect, an example that is reusable; reusable to develop pragmatic, ethical, and political contributions to leadership and learning, learning in organizations, organizational learning; reusable to discover the affective languages of stakeholders, the affective languages of children.

The aim is to overturn authority and power dimensions in knowledge creation processes as well as any anthropomorphic and anthropocentric focus, and instead explore how knowledges and learning emerge, ultimately, to include more and other. Leaders explore how to renew knowledge through collective open-ended processes that, at the same time, ultimately involve the risk of losing what we currently base our practices on, what we currently value, what we sense and regard as sensible. This implies a risk of reopening questions of "who knows how to know" in our learning organizations: leaders interacting with openings toward the futures that are created:

> When we write and can read what we have written for one another; when we can read what others have written, we accentuate it. We highlight it and it becomes more concrete and tangible. The written word has more authority and can also be more scary. One might therefore ask oneself: Oh, am I obliged to relate to what I have written? But we have talked about this a lot in our nursery and about us writing here and now – about [how] this is what I think just now; this is how I conceptualize this today; tomorrow it might look differently. The writing here and now is only valid in the moment. Praxis is movement, and then we cannot be static or fixed in neither thinking nor writing. What we think and write is woven into other thoughts and other texts. (Interview with nursery supervisor and leader, September 10, 2015)

5.1   Data Philosophy, Poetry, and Leadership

Data were produced over a period of two years, from 2015 to 2017, in a nursery in Norway. The data consist of a mix of material from interviews with leaders and staff, and microstories and autoethnographic stories written by two nursery leaders. One of these leaders is the overall manager of the nursery, the other being the leader, organizer, and supervisor of the writing processes. The data also include comments and microstories from staff. All were part of this machinery of edupoetic minor gestures, in which things were *felt, desired, and produced* (Andersson et al., 2020). The different texts are data that are put in motion and philosophized over, showing material cultures and materiality, attuning to things within leadership and learning, learning in organizations, organizational learning. Leaderships written with minor words within leadership moments, or about leaders who have to turn up when needed (Reinertsen & Flatås, 2017). Leadership as a moment and pulse for action and for sensing the joy, for example, over the weight of a bucket of sand, moments when you pick up some mess from the floor as a trace of busy hands. Ultimately, showing how engagement in multiplicity can become attractive as a condition for siding with the child and becoming a strong force for change.

We can find poetry in the texts we write. We can use poetry to expand on our repertoires of techniques and methods in our effort to write our own. When we write and read poems in a group or a nursery, we create duets between leaders and participants, leading and learning, and we are on the road to create relations and connections, and knowledge is possibilized. Poetry allows participation in ideas, moments of, and thoughts about. Poetry invites engagement and activism. Poetry challenges traditional ways of thinking and is capable of turning us over in new directions like any art form can. Poetry can maximize meaning, create new poetry, and cut out the redundant and loud. Poetry inspires respect and attention to other stories and stories of other. Poetry is a way to lay bare the connections between words and the world, proposing an innovative view of texts as expression and action, and of reading/writing as an act of acknowledgment in/for/as leaderships and knowledge creation.

Composing organizational poeticizing practices and ethology implies constant reconquering of traces of events of becomings without organizing these becomings into a certain logics or adopting a narrative aspect. It is an exploration of how a poetic moment in which feelings, importance, and meanings are liberated and sensational becomings continue to work. The poem through this has the ability to transform one event into another and we can talk of navigating in life and of poetic leadership for quality and innovation. Innovation with unplanned moments in the daily work. A choice of leadership expertise in context. Leadership within complexity. Poets as leaders potentializing X through focusing on the multiple character of iterative processes and not its possibility of returning to what used to be.

Leadership and the tasks for leaders and educators in every case are to discover the libidinous or sublime speech of the body and its investments at the social area, with possible internal conflicts between. Relations with and to preconscious or unconscious investments in the same area and then again possible conflicts between these, or rather the whole inter-intra-play between machinic desire and the suppression of desire. Leadership and education seen as an in-phenomenological accelerating and real nonteleological revolution, body as profession in lifegiving insecurity and resistance. Perhaps we can speak of creating polyconsensus organizations in which we recreate ourselves and our pedagogies, institutions, and systems again and again, to not lose force to create on the basis of knowledge.

> Writing makes clearer and "concludes." We all have the same mandate so to speak. And then we ask one another: What does it mean to you, that which you have written? What does it mean for you, that which she/he has written? What does it mean for us when we do this writing together?

> Something happens within us when we write. Not within everybody, but many of us. Some things are hard to write. Some people think it is difficult and hard to pursue a thought. A thought is very strong when standing on a piece of paper in front of you. One can actually become quite frightened over what one has written. Also, what one wrote was not necessarily what one actually thought about this thing that one wrote, about that theme or that issue.

> We also have a few people who have no training in writing at all. For some this gets very scary and felt like some sort of exam in order to produce a result. Many of those who have experienced this as exciting however, now take the initiative to write themselves: "I write this down no. I think it is OK to have it in front of me."

> What we experienced after some time, was that we were very touched by what we wrote. We sensed that we had very strong feelings tied to our respective practical experiences. We had strong feelings attached to it, both in situations when something happened, but also when we talked about it. We cried. Why were we so affected? Why were we so enthusiastic? We did not find any direct answers, but we sat there wondering: What is happening with us? What goes on in this room now and between us, in you, in me? It was left hanging there, and we did not explore it further, but we kept on writing. What we gradually discovered was that the writing opened our eyes. We discovered that the ECE [early childhood education] was another place than what we thought it was. It was almost as if we stretched the

frames around the realities we were part of. Our nursery world became bigger for us than what it was earlier. We became part of something bigger than ourselves. (Interview with nursery supervisor and leader, September 10, 2015)

5.2   Strengthening of the Nursery as a Pedagogical Institution, and Leadership through Writing as Transgressive Method

The nursery I write about here wanted to explore whether writing as transgressive method could strengthen the nursery as a pedagogical institution by bringing forward the best in every employee through written transgressions; and most importantly, innovation and change without losing sight of the child. Transgressions in this perspective, and theorized in Chapter 4, are seen in a processual perspective in which change happens in practice when we understand something new or see realities differently through written approaches. These are processes that visualize and open up nuances, principles, dilemmas, and paradoxes that professionals face, and ambivalence and critique are used as productive approaches to a constant rewriting of practices and services. Critique, if we continue to use that word, is about neither legitimate nor justified criticism per se, but a form of life or a confirmative immanent critique praxis through a state of virtuality in which one asks questions about quality, procedural truthfulness, learning, and justice, and resisting normative ways of thinking and understanding always. Far from being negative or dangerous, this is a chance to create knowledges through invitational transcurricular pedagogies in different process ontologies and, through this, with force to form and stimulate exploration and innovation: Positive difference exceeding all categories. The task of leaders and leading being/becoming primarily to intensify participants' rights as knowers, not what a program or a leader want anyone to know and how.

The nursery in question challenges existing conceptualizations and current practices. It welcomes difference, expansions, and diffractions. It wishes to counter stories as confessions of truths. Rather, the nursery seeks to open up for doubt their insecurities and critical explorations, to access creative, productive, and displacing processes that allow adjustments and supplements in the nursery's practices.

5.2.1   A Magical Fountain

That morning I was out early with only two of the toddlers. It was quiet, no other children, no toys, clean pages. The weather is great, sunny, and dry, but there is a lot of water in our mud pond. Very often, the first professional out empties or brushes the pond away to avoid the children getting wet.

The three of us walk over to the shed to collect buckets and spades. Finn takes the big transparent bucket. Nice for playing with water. I know that Finn loves water. I bring some small windmills too. By the pond the two children become preoccupied by filling the big bucket with water. They use their spades. They work a long time. I collect a milk box to sit on. We talk about filling the bucket all up. Perhaps it can take six or eight litres. More children now dressed for outdoors come and join us. Suddenly there are a lot of children around the pond, especially around the bucket. There are lots of spades and hands. I grab a small bucket to help.

Then something magical happens: The bucket leaks from four holes around the brim. A great fountain is created. The holes are spread evenly and the water spray is symmetric. Both the kids and I get very excited. We shout and laugh together and more children join in. Then the water spray slowly disappears. I yell that we have to fill the fountain with more water. The children get busy. Everybody helps. I get the impression that they all understand the connections: the more water in the bucket, the bigger and stronger water spray. Finn and Bjarne collect cups to capture water sprays, Nina works relentlessly to fill up the bucket. Mari must stir in the bucket all the time and she loses her spade in the "deep" water. Bjarne gets the idea that he can stop the water spray, he feels around one of the holes with his finger. I ask, "Can you stop the water, Bjarne?" He nods and puts his fingers in the hole. Several similar situations occur.

Spontaneously an experimentational play with water emerges. I see small children's explorations and conceptualization processes of mathematics, water pressure and volume. This game lasted a long time and more and more children joined us. I sensed that they were in some sort of flux. This was about the children's own discoveries and something fantastic happened through their experimentations. Simultaneously I ask myself what possibilities we create for the children during outdoor playtime.

We talk a lot about staying in the open with the children to sense their expressions in order for such small experimentations as the one with the fountain to emerge. But, what do we actually offer children for them to wonder about things together? Do we, the staff, manage just to be there with them, without disturbing them, count them or give any odd messages? How engaged are we together with the children, and do they get a feeling of importance when seen by one of the pedagogues? Perhaps this water fountain gets even more important when I print the pictures that I shot and let the children present their discoveries to others.

I am close to the children and their experiences. It is the way I want my relations with the children should be. I do not always manage, but I feel that this is exactly what my mission in relation with the children is. (Micronarrative of general manager, 2017)

5.2.2 Comments from the General Manager

Such important stories as this one are written and shared in every department. Primarily they are shared between colleagues, but they are a fantastic source for me as manager and leader to learn from and get a grip of how close and sensitive the professionals manage to be during hectic days in our nursery, in which time senses and engagement must be shared between many children and many events. I ask myself how I as leader can contribute to the stories and the questions that are posed, contribute to more questions being posed, shared, and experienced, and posing questions as a necessary way of working. Must I as leader always hold on to and keep alive asking questions as a way of working for continuous improvements and through that trigger the huge potential that lies in sharing stories?

Written stories affirm the storyteller toward colleagues and enhance the beliefs in their own practices. They potentialize expanded conceptualizations, and in turn this creates quality for the children. The stories give colleagues opportunities to see each other in a different light. See a colleague who is able to observe, sense and act in micro moments of a child's physical, psychological, and intellectual development. And most important, the stories can light up the individual child when we together with the storyteller go back in time to create an image of what happened with a deeper engagement and empathy. Many of our staff say that the stories help them experience the individual child in a deeper more profound way, and that they through this manage to see, support, exist and participate in important situations for and with the child.

A wished-for practice is when professionals, if absent, call a colleague and inform them about any small thing or appointment they have with a child. The respect and the ability to see and take care of small things and events on behalf of and with a child is important and is the foundation for the quality we create.

5.3 Organization and Leadership Structure

The nursery in question has consciously worked with different forms of leaderships in order to create a distinct culture for exploration and sharing (see the current organizational structure in Figure 5.1). These are forms of

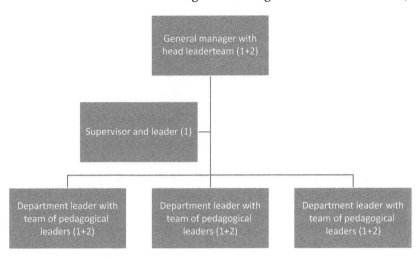

Figure 5.1 Nursery's organizational structure.

leadership inspired by distributed leaderships with a focus on shared responsibilities in organizations, and pedagogical or instructional leaderships with a strong focus on field specific knowledge and competence as basis for good leadership; further, transformational leaderships in which the leader role is that of being inspiring and concentrating efforts to work with relations between leaders and staff; and finally, collaborative leaderships focusing on leading learning in organizations and democracy, hence leaders with a strong focus on participation and autonomy of staff. All forms of leadership or leadership trends can therefore be said to form a sort of backcloth for the nursery in question when they have chosen writing as method and means for change, ultimately for quality. However, expanding via affect, hence going beyond the known, expands on all sources of inspiration and trends to include more.

Through writing, knowledge circulates in the organization and gives a lift to self-creative competence. That in turn creates structures that give leeway to the open and unfinished. All staff members are organized in supervised writing groups in which viewing early childhood in general, and the nursery in question specifically, as a translocal or transformational place is pivotal: as a place for transgression, a place in which to supply new images of what this nursery is and might become. Through critique, practice (hence experience) becomes transparent, and coincidental and "private" practices are avoided.

After several years of writing, staff in this nursery have moved from safe writing and writing success stories to focus on and write what "we do not succeed with" (Fieldnotes, September 2015). Their anchoring of their practices, experience, and conceptualization of change have moved into places of joy and enthusiasm, of humbleness, modesty, and patience; ultimately allowing themselves always to be underway; staying in the open and unfinished.

5.4   A Thinking Meeting, Think Tank Model

The nursery organizes fifty employees in twelve supervised writing groups, one for every department. The writing groups organize themselves, but get one hour with the supervisor every month. Everyone writes from their own position and about something they wonder about and want to expand on. This is a break with established knowledge, hence general, fast, and cumulative knowledge production, by inviting divergent knowledges and questions that interfere with these advancements. Rather, it involves taking people's concerns seriously and paying attention to what is emerging in the moment, and what feels important. To underline, however, this must not be equated with organizations taking account of all messy complications in their environment. Rather, it is about opening up the organization for collective learning through encounters and including dissenting voices around issues of common concern. This entails dissolution of previous structures and hierarchies at the same time as letting novel uncertainties emerge. Again, it is about trying to understand things we still do not know anything about, things that at the first glimpse may seem precarious and which do not make any sense, and from which perhaps arise novel relations that brings us together in unforeseen ways and extends into the future, working and writing of processes of common decency, sensitivity, and relation-making.

> As we have progressed, we have gone from being primarily concerned about themes that we wanted to be more secure of. We have wished to know what we are doing, and how we could recognize what we are doing as learning – or is that learning I now wonder? Can we define it as that, or reduce it to that? Then something happened. Through writing many of our staff discovered new things about their own thinking. Many felt it rather often and wanted to write more and more. Apparently, it opened something up and now if something turns up we say to each other: "Write it down. Write down what you think about now!". (Interview with nursery supervisor and leader, September 10. 2015)

The nursery has formulated four principles for its writing, and how it wants to write:

1.   Low threshold writing and writing stories: All writing is open. No narrative structures are needed. We write without specific genres. We

allow unfinished stories, stories of wonder, a picture, a painting, jokes, questions or just one word.

2. Writing is thinking: Our writing and/as meetings are our thinking meetings. We professionalize with/in our thinking meetings.

3. Supervision and leadership through writing is a two-sided story: activities are systematized through a clear structure in which critique and analysis are characterized by deconstructions, diffraction, refraction, explorations, and experimentations (see Figure 5.2).

4. Evaluation of quality: Resistance is pivotal turning evaluation into learning

> There has been a move from "Oh no!" to "I have written two stories today because I had so much that I wanted to say and write about." A lot is produced. We have developed an alternative professional language. Our efforts have professionalized our work. I now hear that language lives in our corridors: "Do you think that this has anything to do with X? When I say this or that, can you understand it in that way?" People wonder about things together in their everyday practical work and use another type of language than they used to. They ask questions like: "Do you think I defined that child now? What do you think about what I did?" We have developed a richer language that I think contributes positively to our work. Our conversations are characterized by something other than before. Earlier we talked about "Who will do what?" It is almost a move from a more didactical way of talking to an exploration of contents. And we try to position ourselves in a theoretical framework. That has almost become a necessity for us. Theories are in circulation. It is almost like we have developed a need to situate our thinking and wonderings. (Interview with nursery supervisor and leader, September 10, 2015)

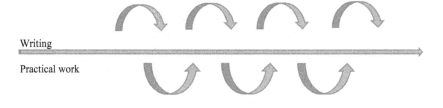

Figure 5.2   Relationship between writing and practical work.

Figure 5.3   Relationship between micronarratives and writing organization.

5.4.1   The General Manager Writes: Our Writing Organization, Our Stops in Flux, and Our Questions

We have been preoccupied with finding ways of working that are effective and enlightening toward our current situation but simultaneously giving directions forward. Our nursery consists of twelve departments with their own leader and leader team. We work across three different facilities or houses. We are successful primarily when everyone systematically and regularly brings in stories that describe the deep play of children and children's thinking and descriptions of how pedagogues tune in to this in ways that support, enrich and don't disturb. We write to, and at, practically all types of meetings. At *week stop meetings*, the children attend. The parents know the drill and are informed about the contents of the meetings and what happened afterward. These meetings take place either Friday afternoon or Monday morning. Afterward, themes from the week stop meetings with the children are lifted into the supervised writing groups. In these groups, all participants continue writing and through this produce decisive contributions to our constant evaluation of activities for quality at department level.

The week stop meetings help us understand more about the processes the children currently are preoccupied with and engaged in. We also wish for parents to have increased possibilities to have a say in, and influence, our pedagogical processes and the choices we make on behalf of children. Another thing we wish for is to increase our focus on the importance of nurseries and the inherent value of childhood. Many competent parents and grandparents can now access our activities, and we experience that our collaboration with parents improves when the pedagogues and staff facilitate and invite them into conversations about the contents of week stop meetings. We also encourage parents to contribute with their own competences in accordance with their own professional backgrounds, interests, or hobbies. We experience that parent engagement and understanding increase concurrently with their opportunities to read themselves into our activities.

Parallel with, and as an integrated part of writing, we arrange an evaluation stop every fourth week to amass the last four *weekstops*. Then we ask ourselves the following questions:

1. What have we been preoccupied with, explored, and wondered about, and how do we pursue it further? What has it contributed with and to, and produced for the individual child and the group of children?
2. How have we used the week stop meetings: as a tool for innovation with children and in communication with parents . . .? What have we discovered through the *weekstops* that we can bring with us further in our organization and planning?
3. How would you describe your own engagement with and contribution together with children?

By assembling four weekstops, we get an overview over processes and activities the children have been preoccupied with in the last month or so and always with a view to what we speak of as *justice in the moment*. Just as important as what we have documented through writing, however, is what we have not documented, forgotten, not prioritized and valued. That way of working contributes to transparency, but as more than what we have experienced before. It opens up for what all staff in one way or the other must focus on in the time that comes.

Life in kindergarten is complex, and consists mainly of decision-making in relation to what every staff member must and can prioritize in every humane relation throughout the day. It demands flexible practices by us all. The whole personnel group must be prepared to make new decisions and prioritize which traces to follow at any time. Quite naturally new questions constantly pop up: Is it risky to make even more of our activities transparent for parents? Will we enforce their expectations, and will we experience even greater performance pressure?

In addition to monthly evaluations, we have biannual evaluations that are more comprehensive. Then we pick examples from every Monthly Schedule or Plan and make assemblages of texts and pictures for retro-flection, evaluation, and summing up. We experience that this way of working has positive effects as far as visualizing more clearly the kind of decisions we make on children's behalves. We also pose reflection-questions and additional or support questions based on our overall Year Plan:

1. What have we discovered and experienced the last six months that have produced importance for our pedagogical work?
2. What connections do we see between our pedagogical work and our visions and goals?
3. What must we prioritize the next six months?

Every department leader decides what questions to forward, and what to discuss and debate in their own teams concurrently. Every leader must have an active relation to the questions and be able to work with them on behalf of the group of children and the team of professionals she leads. When all the teams at department level have completed their biannual evaluations, the work for the manager and my team of leaders begins for real. We read all the reports from the twelve departments and discuss how to respond to and support the departments in their efforts. The main point with the evaluation is learning what the nursery as a pedagogical endeavor should be. Equally important though is that leaders realize their responsibilities as to what and how to support the different departments and consider which new and other questions we need to ask in order to create professional practices. Every staff member must take part and experience these processes in order for us subsequently to involve parents and owners in the same evaluation processes.

> Reality in ECE can be brutal and we must dare to talk aloud about what we do not succeed in or with. Then we also need leaders who are receptive for those kinds of stories. (Interview with nursery supervisor and leader, September 10, 2015)

Through organizing writing groups, we have established a leadership arena for awareness and exploration. Leaders at all levels are trained in running processes at their own departments. Every group starts with the supervisor present, but gradually their own respective leaders take over and lead their own groups. Writing is therefore linked to the pedagogical goals that are set but also to specific leadership goals. Working consciously and integrally with leadership is part of our policy. We want to create importance for individuals, departments, pedagogical practices, and our organization alike. As far as the organization is concerned, through writing we unveil development needs, support, and potentials. All in all, this increases transparency in our organization. We experience that staff presence and sensitivity in proximity with children increases. We also experience greater enthusiasm and curiosity toward impacts and the policy mandate of Early Childhood Education and Care (ECEC) in general. The way we work and the writing does *something*. Both individual and collective shifts are visible.

Through this, the leaders get enhanced opportunities to observe and discuss with the whole personnel, what to focus on and study both individually and collectively at department levels. In addition, we get a better grip on what our organization as a whole needs as far as increase in competences and further development. A very important task for leaders is to lead processes of critical reflections, be a role model and encourage production of observations and stories, participate in writing, and always take notes.

What we want is to challenge the traditional pedagogies and policies of our nurseries and create openings toward continuous disturbances in order to avoid doing what we always have done. We want to avoid reproducing knowledges and actions and open up for that *something* between. Open up between what *is* and what might *become*. We want to disturb habits and break with the streamlining of practices in which one just goes with the flow without being conscious of the discursive flows one acts with/in and through. We want to create space for actions that disturb the self-evident and the taken for granted, avoid reproducing the same. What we have not done is search for objective truths, but through disturbances, we have tried to open up for new perspectives to continue thinking *with* the child. We focus more on contents than methods in the processes and genreless experimentations have been vital and our "hub," so to speak.

We have discovered that the world in the kindergarten is something else and much more than what we used to think. Our forms of work and writing in themselves contribute to a wish to expand on what we think are the frames of the realities we are part of. This way our situated realities are resuscitated repeatedly. Evaluation of our work has been given another format and appears time-saving. Further, this gives us room to reconceptualize our practices through developing a more holistic approach to the processes we are in. The value of experimentations and mental mobility make us strong. Through systematic mentoring and/as writing we see interaction between critical reflexivity, *weekstops* and evaluation. The processes are interdependent. Writing coincides with documentation of pedagogical activities and become simultaneously method and means in any types of projects we now initiate and continue to develop.

> We have developed a richer language that I think contributes big time to our practices. Our conversations are marked with something different from before. Then we talked about who does what. We have moved from an almost didactical way of speaking to wondering about contents. And we try to place ourselves in a theoretical framework. It is almost as if that has become an urge of ours. (Interview with nursery supervisor and leader, September 10, 2015)

Through writing, we have experienced that working with improvements and innovation has moved from being a duty to becoming a necessity. The personnel express enthusiasm and a strong urge to continue with the writing. One starts to realize one's own value for the nursery kindergarten and the mandate we are given. Further, writing creates a clearer perspective of our own practices both in retrospect and in foresight, a belief in our own forces: brave, open and competent. It strengthens beliefs in our own capacities to change.

Our nursery has allocated resources for one internal supervisor, but with a mission to spread and share supervision competences with all department and pedagogical leaders. Supervision is a type of leadership in our organization. We chose one particular theme every six months, and for us this has contributed to strengthening harmonic relations between supervisors and the supervised. Harmony understood as the establishment of a culture in which it is safe to challenge and stretch words, concepts, and attitudes. There is an important interaction between following the child, affect and being affected and simultaneously holding on systematic and good ways of working. What shall we focus on in writing, and in what light shall we see what we write? Every professional makes many decisions every hour, every day and week, and for that we must be equipped again and again. As head I work hard in order for every employee to sense the value of his/her own experiences and sensations hence the value of putting it in motion. That gives energy, courage, and a will to act. The value of experimentations and explorations creates force so that the joy of meeting the child here and now makes us curious about what we can do and be together. A conductor without a score will fall short without hearing, genuine interest, intonation, and tonality for flux and meaning making. Writing in supervised writing groups is the score of the pedagogue.

Here are some micronarratives from staff:

> Writing increases my motivation, give me new ideas and more *do* power. It supports me in the priorities I make during hectic days of work.

> I become more aware of things when it is picked up in writing.

> We build confidence and create knowledges ourselves.

> We build confidence and create knowledge ourselves.

> The structure is OK. Good evaluations, good conclusions leading to something, everyone's voice counts: equality.

> We start with what is, an overriding theme based on a pedagogical practice which is already there.

> I see practice from new angles. Writing helps me expand my perspectives. Many questions challenge. There are many aha moments.

> We get closer to each other and open up for learning. We are not afraid to fail.

> I like the supervision of the writing groups. It redeems our practices.

> The writing is a charger; we can lower our shoulders and focus on communication.

> I have become braver, and we have developed an emotional closeness to one another.

The general manager continues:

The way I see this, we have some opinions, cognitions, and questions that we have to pose and think through very thoroughly. The first concerns avoiding searching for the one and only truth. The second is about seeing the kindergarten as a contested place and interesting phenomena instead of defending safe and familiar practices. Do we dare ask those questions? Do we dare be critical to our own practices? Are we able to go deep enough, challenge our weak spots and ourselves? Do we allow ourselves to be affected on behalf of the children? Do we search enough for the hard questions?

> Through this work, we have become braver. We rehearse moving out of our comfort zones. We increase insight in each other's practices and this makes us safe to share with one another. We are challenged to explore doubts and

always wonder more in order to turn off the autopilot. Seen this way, we all have to take responsibility for reaching our goals together. (Micronarrative of general manager, 2017)

Types of questions that we ask ourselves are:

What happens when we challenge established truths?
How insecure do we dare be? What do we risk?
What would be better practices than what we perform today?
How do we do reflexivity in the/every moment, and not just in organized meetings?

5.4.2   Leadership and Supervision: The General Manager and the Supervisor

Collaboration between manager and supervisor is vital. Together, and through continuous evaluation, we have discussed examples for circulation in our organization, examples that can create new transitions, with and for the children. Procedural conditions are discussed to create room for support and quality assurance individually, of every team and department. We would have preferred to spend even more time on digging deeper, search for more good examples and to be able to support the teams earlier. As manager and supervisor, we could have listened to each other more often with a view to explore even more perspectives for composing a learning organization. The manager must know the qualities of the organization, every child's possibility to thrive and explore, play and learn. With the stories, the written examples, we create a better and trustworthy base for moving the personnel through expanded processes and support the dialogs and critical assessments when things sometimes get difficult. The knowledge that the manager needs to do this is mainly produced in meetings between manager and supervisor. It is of great value for the manager that the supervisor has profound knowledge about the organization's inner life.

> I think of myself as leader in supervision. But what might be a little different is that the road is built while we walk it. I need to dare that the future is open for us. If we are to reach what we are required to do, we need to change some of the contents- but also how we conceptualize ourselves as an organization. We need to talk about leadership again. Leadership is no longer division of roles and tasks, who is in charge of what and who bakes the bread, but how we can run the kindergarten as a first step in lifelong learning. If that is the case, what is the most appropriate way of running our organization, and what do we then need to talk about? (Interview with nursery supervisor and leader, September 10, 2015)

As leaders we work actively for opening up for new and more gazes on everyday realities. How can we support each other through using our own lives and experiences in order to become better pedagogues for the children? How can we set ourselves in motion and write meaning forward? How can we create knowledge together, what can we agree on and simultaneously agree that nobody knows anything for certain? How can we spend our thoughts for better understanding?

> I think I challenge people to critically reflect on what we traditionally have done, [rather] than just asking them to reflect on what we traditionally have done. That is asking more than [to] just reflect. I open up for the thought that if we are going to be something else than what we are today, what do we then do? I structure my supervision the way [so] that everybody [has] to get involved and contribute. (Interview with nursery supervisor and leader, September 10, 2015)

Composing a learning organization through writing in supervised writing groups is a way of working to connect national policies with the particular practices of local nurseries. We are moving toward a procedural based development and leadership model in which we, through writing, enable ourselves to adapt, translate, connect supply and demand knowledge, catalyze, and facilitate. Tensions between the internal and external produce new horizons. That includes the possibility to reject external leadership programmes and courses in order to secure integrated, internal, and long perspectives.

The child and the pedagogues' ability of endurance, sensation, respect and engagement for the individual person affects me. The child becomes visible for the group, and a skilled leader and pedagogue makes new affirmations in the meeting with the child which probably will continue its influence on her, always viewing the child differently. The conscious leader lifting herself further. And this might be what I think of as an exemplary principle. (Micronarrative of general manager, 2017)

> Writing is risking value increase. Practice increases its value through writing. This is because you make new discoveries, which release pictures of the nursery that you did not even realize existed. That while simultaneously discovering your own value and importance. The little things that I do increase in value.

February: It is before noon and the oldest children have gone out. The smaller ones are inside and they use the whole nursery. I enter The Magic Flute and Leonora walks towards me. She looks at me and lifts up two pink Lego walls. She tries to say something, but I cannot understand her. I look at her and ask if she wants us to build with the Legos? She smiles and points her finger towards where the rest of the Legos are. We walk over together to find more Legos. We start building and Leonora finds even more Legos. Soon after Liam joins in and also he brings more Legos. Liam also wants to build with Legos.

Finally, the house we build is finished and Liam suddenly gets very energetic. He puts different Lego figures and Legos through the door. Leonora goes along with it and they take figures in and out of the house. Marianne comes over to help, but Liam does not like that she takes the toys. I say: "Maybe Marianne also wants to put Lego figures and toys in the house?" Liam looks at me, but says nothing. He continues playing and Marianne is allowed to help. They play with the house for some time, but then they are not interested any more and they walk away to find something else.

Reflections: I think the way I meet Leonora creates play. I could have just said "Oh do you have Legos? They are nice and pink." But that would not have contributed to the play and I think Leonora would not have felt that she was seen and understood. It is easy during a busy day to meet children like this. You see the child and you name what you see, but without following up what you see. I wonder what that does to the child.

I think that Leonora senses that I understand her and that she manages to make contact with another human being when I meet her the way I do. I also think that this situation creates interplays between several children and they experience something nice together. Something else or third emerges together with another. Later that day I observed Liam and Leonora playing with cars together. I ask myself if perhaps the play with Legos earlier had created a connection between them, or...? (Interview with nursery supervisor and leader, September 10, 2015)

5.4.3   Comments from the General Manager

One child 100 languages ... I think this professional makes some very important observations. She reflects over the power of words and can, through this, open up for different activities and solutions. She succeeds in including three two-year olds in a fine collaborative play. In addition, she shows the ability to perspectivize by making a situation transparent and open for herself and her colleagues in writing as thinking meetings in which this story was shared and reflected over. She experienced and assumed that children take up positive experiences and make use of them in new situations. Competences and friendships are built. She poses a beautiful and open question and makes room for doubt. I chose to believe that every employee who shares such important microstories, moves on and chases new verbal and nonverbal expressions in which children create new knowledge through their actions.

We write ourselves toward more formulations that are precise and conceptualizations of both what we know and what we don't know. We ask again and again:

How do we work with becoming?
How do we explore more?
What can we do more of?
What should we stop doing?
How do we spot a child in difficulties, not with difficulties?
What are our concerns in the department or our group now?
What is your concern, your questions?

CHAPTER 6

A Cultural-Historical Activity Theory Perspective on Learning to Lead

Joce

This chapter describes a conceptual framework drawn from cultural-historical activity theory (CHAT) as a third potential approach to theorizing processes of learning and development, with an emphasis on learning to lead. CHAT originates in Marxian psychologies of collective labor so, in this chapter, leadership in early childhood education is understood as a form of collaborative thinking across collective work. Throughout this chapter, this standpoint will provide a counterpoint to claims about leaders' work that anchor practices of leadership in individual psychological processes such as beliefs and dispositions. The Marxian psychological origins of CHAT also mean that leadership work, when seen from a CHAT perspective, cannot be separated from the political and economic work of early childhood education.

Before outlining key concepts, the chapter describes the origins of CHAT in the work of L. S. Vygotsky (1896–1934) and his collaborators, particularly A. N. Leontiev (1903–1979). CHAT is one branch of a group of related theoretical perspectives that share their origins in Marxian thought. In the first part of the chapter, I introduce some of the concepts that members of this family share, including the concept of internal "contradictions" (both within individuals and within systems) as the stimulus for change and development. In the second part of the chapter, I describe the practice-developing methodology known as Change Laboratory (Virkkunen & Newnham, 2013). Change Laboratory mobilizes concepts from CHAT to collaboratively design changes in work practices, while simultaneously documenting the learning and development evidenced through these changes. This approach means it lends itself well to thinking about practices of leadership, as well as thinking about the development of leaders. Change Laboratory was the approach used in the work with Haneul Early Learning Center (this is a pseudonym), the early childhood service described in Chapter 7, as it sought to develop its approach to workplace induction and support for new members of its teaching team.

6.1 CHAT and Marxian Psychology

CHAT is part of a *"collaborative, multi-generational, value-laden, and ideologically-driven investigative project"* (Stetsenko, 2003, p. 96, italics in original) originating in the work of L. S. Vygotsky and his fellow psychologists in Russia in the first half of the twentieth century. Other members of this family of theories include sociocultural theory, sociohistorical theory, activity theory, and cultural-historical theory. Although there are some important differences between these theories, they share at least three core commitments.

First, they reject behaviorist explanations for human learning and development. Stimulus-response psychology and techniques of classical conditioning, originating in the work of I. P. Pavlov (1849–1936), were in the ascendant internationally in the late nineteenth century. For Marxists, however, explanations that promoted an essentially individualist notion of human life were not only theoretically inadequate; they were also ideologically uncomfortable – even dangerous – in the context of communitarian life in the Soviet Union of the early twentieth century.

Second, researchers in the cultural-historical project originating with Vygotsky follow his original impetus of striving to develop an objectively scientific method of studying the mind in the context of social situations (the title of his best-known work in its English translation is *Mind in Society* [Vygotsky, 1978]). An important aim of researchers in this tradition is to understand the complex interplay, found in social situations, between historically accumulating cultural processes and human development across time.

Third, researchers in the CHAT tradition are united in an intellectual project that is not only empirical but political. Following Marxian commitments to consciousness-raising and anti-oppressive politics, particularly for vulnerable and disadvantaged communities, researchers in the Vygotskian tradition often work to mobilize the agency and expand developmental possibilities for groups that have historically been disadvantaged. I argue that women working in early childhood education, particularly in childcare, are one such group. This group of workers is also increasingly characterized by the intersectionality of gender, class, and cultural and linguistic diversity. These intersections materialize in the form of poor pay and working conditions, and wear and tear on personal and professional bodies. This is the collaborative context in which many leaders of early childhood services find themselves undertaking their work.

6.2 Key Concepts of CHAT

The scope of this chapter only allows for a brief introduction to each of the concepts we touch on here. Rather than extend our elaboration of theory, we offer examples of workplace phenomena related to leadership in early childhood services to illustrate the ways these concepts might materialize.

6.2.1 Activity

Cultural-historical activity theorists and researchers study the development of human *activity*. Activity is understood both as a psychological function and as an externalization of these functions in the form of observable actions. Early childhood centers are complex *systems* of collaborative activity (*activity systems* in CHAT parlance) that co-evolve (Beach, 1999) with the individual and shared psychological activity of leaders, educators, children, families, and managers. Given that the concept of activity is central to CHAT, as well as to its close relative activity theory, there is an extensive literature debating the nature of activity in this theoretical tradition. For the purposes of this chapter, however, it is useful to think of activity as analogous with *practice*, since activity systems in CHAT are systems of workplace practices.

6.2.2 Internalization and Externalization

As individuals and groups strive to engage in culturally valued collaborative activity, such as early childhood education, they must *internalize* the concepts of this activity. These concepts do not originate within individuals and simply emerge through processes of discovery or maturation. Rather, concepts are held within cultures, so are present *before* individuals or groups enter those cultures. For example, the field of early childhood education has distinctive concepts expressed in practice (e.g., care-as-curriculum [Bussey & Hill, 2017]) that are immediately recognizable to experienced members of the culture of early childhood education, but which have to be learned by novices (such as preservice teachers) who seek to enter into that culture. The work of leaders in early childhood services, particularly if they have unqualified educators in their team, may include introducing educators to concepts that are culturally specific to early childhood education, such as play-based learning, and allied practices. (See Nuttall [2022] for a description of how one Educational Leader introduced the concept of "attachment" to her team to provoke shifts in their practices related to distressed children.)

6.2.3 *Cultural Tools and Signs*

Vygotsky's explanation for how individuals and groups come to internalize these a priori concepts is that they are maintained and conveyed through *cultural tools and signs*. Cultural tools are externally oriented (i.e., they have an observable practical use), while signs are internally (psychologically) oriented. The connection between the internal and the external is explained as a *dialectical* relationship between ontogenesis – the way individuals develop through their lives – and phylogenesis – the development of humanity as a whole across history. The argument that individual minds and collective societies simultaneously develop each other was a major breakthrough in theories of psychology. Vygotsky's argument that "[M]an's alteration of nature alters man's own nature" (Vygotsky, 1978, p. 55) was truly revolutionary in the early twentieth century. In essence, it is an argument for the capacity of humans to change themselves and their world *from the outside* by inventing and adapting the meanings-in-use of cultural tools (Daniels, 2001).

This emphasis on the meaning-carrying and meaning-conveying nature of cultural tools explains why individuals internalize the meanings and use of concepts and cultural tools that are valued by their community. Yet early childhood education still struggles to identify leadership-related concepts and practices that are appropriate to the field. This has been due, in part, to the tendency to look to schools and concepts of principalship for direction, despite the important systemic differences – professional, historical, and industrial – in the activities that define schools in contrast to early childhood services.

6.2.4 *Mediation*

Early childhood education services are rich with cultural tools in the form of concepts that, taken as a whole, provide the cultural context for work in early childhood education. For educators, these concepts include "play-based learning," "intentional teaching," "learning," "development," "caregiving," "planning," and "assessment." These concepts are externalized through distinctive cultural tools and through material artifacts, such as planning templates and daily diaries, that *mediate* observable pedagogical practices. Within CHAT, mediation is the process that occurs within the relationship between people and the tasks that direct and give meaning to their psychological development. In the absence of concepts originating in practices of early childhood education, concepts specific to leaders in early childhood services may include "practice," "performance," "compliance," and/or "teamwork," leading to observable practices of coaching, feedback, and personal persuasion.

For example, an early childhood leader may wish to plan for the development of a group of educators (the educator's object of activity – see Section 6.2.8). To aid in this work, they may take up a cultural tool that has been specifically designed (either in their center or the wider field) to mediate professional development activities; such resources are legion in the early childhood field. But the chosen cultural tool will not be neutral. Engineered into the chosen format will be a rich range of meanings and assumptions from within the professional field (about children, about planning, about learning, about teachers' work, etc.) that are more or less known to the leader using the professional learning resource.

6.2.5 Double Stimulation

This simultaneous process of meeting a practice problem with a cultural tool is known within CHAT as *double stimulation* (Sannino, 2015). This cultural tool, with its built-in meanings, provides a secondary stimulus for the leader facing a practical challenge of closing the gap (the first stimulus) between the situation they currently face and the practices they desire for the center. In other words, the meanings that inhere in the cultural tool chosen by the leader in the example above (e.g., professional judgment, imagined future practices) are brought to the leader's desire to implement effective professional development in the center. Virkkunen and Ristimäki (2012) provide the following definition of double stimulation as originally conceptualized by Vygotsky:

> When studying the mediation of actions, Vygotsky (1978, pp. 72–75) applied the method of *double stimulation*. In it a person is given a problem that exceeds his or her current competence (first stimulus). While the person is trying to solve the problem, another stimulus is brought into the situation. The researcher observes whether the person takes the creative leap of inventing a way of using the provided second stimulus as an instrument in solving the problem. "We might say that when difficulties arise, neutral stimuli take on the function of a sign and from that point on the operation's structure assumes an essentially different character" (Vygotsky, 1978, p. 74). (Virkkunen & Ristimäki, 2012, p. 274, emphasis in original)

Where practices are already mediated by cultural tools, some processes of *remediation* (Miettinen et al., 2012) may also be necessary, that is, adaptation or replacement of a cultural tool to mediate practices anew. Two processes of mediation are possible: explicit mediation and implicit mediation.

6.2.6 Explicit Mediation

Leaders can introduce new cultural tools and their meanings to educators and describe their conceptual basis. This process of deliberate exposure is known as *explicit mediation*:

> First, it is explicit in that an individual, or another person who is directing this individual, overtly and intentionally introduce a "stimulus means" into an ongoing system of activity. Second, it is explicit in the sense that the materiality of the stimulus means, or signs involved, tends to be obvious and non-transitory. (Wertsch, 2007, p. 180)

Although approaches to professional development may vary across early childhood services, the design and meanings of cultural tools are relatively stable and, therefore, nontransitory. For example, in the contemporary era of persistent discourses of program quality, many governments publish national standards that purport to provide stable meanings of aspects of quality. In the case of Haneul Early Learning Centre, described in Chapter 7, regulations regarding ratios of staff to children as well as workplace agreements about working hours continued to mediate the Educational Leaders' work, even as they attempted to change staffing practices.

6.2.7 Implicit Mediation

But what about leaders who have not been exposed to explicit mediation in their learning about approaches to professional development for their teams? Does this mean such leaders are incapable of fostering change in their early childhood services? Since many leaders who have not been schooled in principles of professional learning or adult learning theory *do* foster the learning of colleagues, another process of meaning-making for these leaders must be in play. Most likely, they have experienced professional development activities themselves, so have become enculturated to typical systems of professional learning activity, such as team workshops, distribution of professional reading, and invitations to guest speakers. This process of learning from experience is known in CHAT as *implicit mediation.* Implicit mediation is frequently hidden from view, either because it is already internalized (i.e., worked out within an individual mind), or because the tools and signs involved "are part of a pre-existing, independent stream of communicative action that becomes integrated with other forms of goal-directed behaviour" (Wertsch, 2007, p. 181); that is, the activity is already "preconfigured" to guide the actions that comprise and develop from it to produce certain outcomes. Immersion in the everyday sayings and doings of a culture, even without explicit mediation, can result in the development of individuals and groups. This is how leaders in early childhood education can make plans for staff development even if they cannot to draw on prior leadership education. Success may be possible because of implicit mediation, even though they may not be able to immediately unpack the meanings or specific concepts that underpin the design of their approach to the development of their colleagues.

6.2.8   *Object of Activity, Motive*

In CHAT terminology, practical demands (the need to plan for educators' learning, in our example) provide the *motive* for *objects of activity*. These "objects" are not tangible "things" in the everyday sense of the objects that surround us, but a focus for practical and psychological activity. Objects of activity give focus and direction to voluntary practical activity (described as *volitional action* by Sannino [2015]), thereby providing the force that draws development forward:

> The main thing which distinguishes one activity from another ... is the difference of their objects. It is exactly the object of an activity that gives it a determined direction. According to the terminology I have proposed, the object of the activity is its true motive. (Leont'ev, 1978, p. 62)

In the case of Haneul Early Learning Center in Chapter 7, the leadership team was initially motivated by the need to make the outdoor play area safer for the young children in the center; as work on this object developed, a further object came into view that could resolve multiple issues of safety and other forms of organization; namely, improving the induction of new staff members.

6.2.9   *Conflict of Motives*

This final concept acknowledges that individuals and groups typically have multiple simultaneous objects of activity motivating their practice (both children's safety and good staff induction, in our example), but that they cannot all be given the same priority or level of attention. Leaders in early childhood services, for example, may be simultaneously working with teams to develop approaches to planning, lobbying their governing body for increased resources for professional learning activities, enculturating new or unqualified staff into norms of center practice, and responding to external evaluations of center performance against national standards. The resulting struggle to determine a priority order of objects of activity is known as a *conflict of motives* (Morselli & Sannino, 2021). This conflict is neither predictable nor stable, since the items given highest priority at any one time will depend on a wide range of contextual variables at play. These might include the time available for dedicated leadership work, the priority given to particular objects of activity by center management, the tolerance of the staff team in relation to the speed of change, and resources available to the leader, such as time and materials for their own leadership development. There is evidence, for example, that new leaders in early childhood services prioritize learning about administrative and managerial aspects of center leadership over the development of pedagogical practice (Whalley, 2011).

A leader's choices of which motive to pursue is also unstable because it is determined not just by practical challenges that form motivating objects of activity but by the emotional character of motivating objects. A leader may know that their priority *should* be to solve a particular practice problem among a group of staff, but they may fear that they will lose the friendly relationships they have developed with this group by attempting to intervene in center practices. Such tensions are nontrivial in workplace settings, such as early childhood services, that can only function well when a positive emotional tone prevails among staff, children, and families. Leaders experience such situations both as personal professional dilemmas and as systemic tensions that interfere with the fulfillment of motivating objects. I return to the nature and function of these tensions, known conceptually within CHAT as *contradictions*, in Section 6.4. Before doing so, I turn to the way CHAT researchers and interventionists in workplace practices view *collective practice* as an analytic unit.

6.3   The Nature of Activity "Systems"

Some researchers in the Vygotskyan tradition focus on the psychological development of individuals at various life stages, and the dynamic between learners and their social contexts. CHAT researchers pay attention to the ways in which *collective subjects* (groups of persons) achieve complex objects of activity by using mediational means to organize their work. This focus stems from A. N. Leontiev's theory of collective activity. Leontiev argued that groups' fulfillment of their objects is mediated by *rules*, which guide group values and protocols, and a *division of labor*, which dictates who takes responsibility for which tasks related to specific objects, so that groups can achieve their ultimate *outcomes*.

For example, leaders in early childhood services may be working on multiple objects of activity – reassuring parents, giving feedback to educators, designing or adapting cultural tools such as planning templates – and each of these tasks will be conducted according to the leader's understanding of her place in the division of labor and the rules that govern the work of the center. Some of these rules and divisions of labor will be implicit, but through experience of working in the center (and as a leader), the individual knows what is expected of her. However, while these tasks may be understood in discrete ways, they come together in the interests of the overall outcome that early childhood services aim to achieve, that of educating and caring for young children in ways that increase the likelihood of those children flourishing now and in the future.

Figure 6.1 (Engeström, 1987) is a diagrammatic representation of the relationship between outcomes, objects, and the various mediational

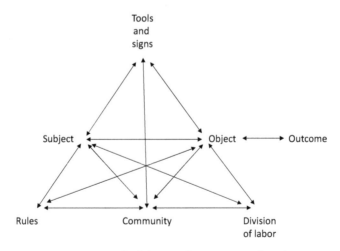

Figure 6.1   Basic structure of collaborative human activity (based on Engeström, 1987, p. 78).

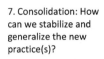
7. Consolidation: How
can we stabilize and
generalize the new
practice(s)?

1. Questioning: What is
the need state that has
arisen in practice?

6. Reflecting on the
process: What has been
learned from the design
and implementation of
the new practice(s)?

2. Analysis: What is the
'double bind' that is
hindering practice?

5. Implementing the new
model: What ongoing
modifications are
needed?

3. Modelling the solution:
What potential
breakthroughs might
resolve the double bind?

4. Examining and testing
the model: What happens
when we try the new
solution in practice?

Figure 6.2   Expansive learning cycle (adapted from Engeström, 1999, p. 384).

means at play in collective work. Crucially, Leontiev showed how *multiple and simultaneous mediation* gives rise to the dynamic and complex nature of workplaces since, at any one moment, every aspect shown in Figure 6.1 is mediating every other aspect. This means that workplaces will always tend toward change and instability, even as distinctive practices continue as enduring features of particular professions.

Engeström's (1987) addition of *community* to this representation (Figure 6.1) acknowledges the way the perspectives of close stakeholders also mediate collaborative work settings such as early childhood centers.

Engeström also went on to show how individual activity systems never operate in isolation but are also influenced by adjacent activity systems. For example, an early childhood service may operate largely as a separate entity in practice but still experience incoming disturbances from Departments of Education (or other regulatory bodies), overarching corporate bodies (if the center is part of a corporate provider), or schools that enroll children from the center once they reach school age.

As the arrows in Figure 6.1 illustrate, every aspect of an activity system mediates every other aspect. This means that changes to one aspect of mediation can change the whole system. For example, introduction of a new approach to assessing and reporting children's learning (a cultural tool) requires that teams also work out the rules for its use (How many assessments will be made? Will each child receive the same number of assessments?) and the division of labor (Who will make the assessments? Who will report educators' judgments to families?). New cultural tools may be introduced in good faith, but without attention to how they remediate the whole activity system, they may fail to be taken up or, even worse, stimulate unanticipated and problematic disturbances within the system as a whole. These disturbances may not be evident until resistance arises among the team, sometimes evident in a reassertion of existing rules and divisions of labor. It is the work of leaders, therefore, to collaborate with colleagues to thoughtfully and systematically consider, adapt, and renew mediational means in the interests of valued outcomes. Chapter 7 describes an example of how this was achieved at Haneul ELC, including the way center leaders were able to imaginatively hold onto the objects that motivated the changes the center made and how these objects connected to their desired outcomes.

6.4   Activity Systems as Contradictory Sites of Practice

The concept of *contradictions* is central to understandings about practice change within CHAT. In the Marxian tradition, contradictions are not conflicts, but systematic tensions that provide the springboard for generative change; Harvey (2014) describes them as a "point where the stress between opposing desires feels unbearable" (Harvey, 2014, p. 6). Contradictions within activity systems may be evident over long periods of time but, as Harvey suggests, they may eventually become evident in workplaces because they are confounding attempts to achieve valued workplace objects.

Marx's original conceptualization of contradictions related to the relationship between the labor power of workers and the interests of capitalist economies. This has particular implications for work in early childhood education, because of its movement over time from unpaid labor in the home to paid labor outside the home:

> The effect is to transform social labour – the labour we do for others – into *alienated* social labour. Work and labour are exclusively organised around the production of commodity exchange values that yield the monetary return upon which capital builds its social powers of class domination. Workers, in short, are put in a position where they can do nothing other

than reproduce through their work the conditions of their own domination. This is what freedom under the rule of capital means for them. (Harvey, 2014, p. 39; italics in original)

Marx argued that, once the contradictions of capital are brought to conscious awareness, workers will resist the alienation of their labor. Yet this has proved to be more true in theory than in practice for many professions, including early childhood education, where workers are indeed aware of the undervaluing of their work in the interests of capital and have campaigned vigorously for change, to limited effect. As Harvey (2014) goes on to explain:

> There has been a long history, for example, of defining skilled labour in gendered terms such that any task that women could perform – no matter how difficult or complex – was classified as unskilled simply because women could do it. Worse still, women were often allocated these tasks for so-called "natural" reasons (everything from nimble fingers to a supposedly naturally submissive and patient temperament). . . . The fact that there has been an extensive feminisation both of low-wage labour and of poverty worldwide testifies clearly to the importance of these sorts of judgements, for which there is no technical basis whatsoever. (pp. 66–67)

6.5 Systemic Contradictions as a Springboard for Workplace Development

The primary purpose of theorizing contradictions is to understand how they provide the impetus for development. In CHAT analyses, systemic contradictions present themselves in workplaces as unresolved tensions within or between aspects of the system. For example, a rule may contradict another rule, or a rule may be contradicted by the division of labor. Taking the example from Section 6.3 of the development of a new assessment tool: an early childhood center may work out rules and divisions of labor around its use, but if the tool is badly designed (and so does not fulfill the motivating object of activity of better understanding children's learning progression) then contradictions will quickly arise. No recasting of rules and divisions of labor can compensate for a badly designed tool.

When the elements of an activity system are realigned to resolve a contradiction, however, the result is not just achievement of the object motivating the work. The subjects in the system also gain a greater sense of *agency*, that is, the capacity to take volitional action to change their life circumstances. This reflects the way individuals and groups feel more capable and powerful when they can design and adapt their own work processes. The first step, however, is to bring prevailing contradictions into view. In the case of Haneul Early Learning Center, described in Chapter 7, the contradiction was between a rule ("We provide effective induction of new staff") and a prevailing object of activity ("We need to minimize staffing costs"). The outward signs of this contradiction arose when new staff were put immediately to work with colleagues, children, and families, without properly understanding the local cultural norms and work practices of the center. Inevitably, this led to episodes that undercut the smooth operation of the center and, ultimately, did not reduce staffing costs, since more experienced staff ended up having to spend more time with new staff to overcome misunderstandings and explain work practices "on the run." Thus, a contradiction internal to the center system, between a rule and an object, became uncomfortably evident.

CHAT researchers and theorists claim that it is through the resolution of contradictions (and the new contradictions that inevitably arise in the wake of earlier resolutions) that people and institutions develop new forms of workplace practice over time. Some contradictions will always be unresolved, in part because workers rarely have full control of the circumstances in which they do their work. Within CHAT, the enduring presence of contradictions, however, is seen as a positive sign since, without the discomfort felt due to internal contradictions, there is no impetus for change and development.

6.6 Change Laboratory as an Approach to Active Resolution of Systemic Contradictions

The remaining sections of this chapter describe the research and development methodology of Change Laboratory. Change Laboratory is an interventionist approach to research and development developed by Finnish researcher Yrjö Engeström and his colleagues at the University of Helsinki. It seeks to understand workplaces practices at the same time as fostering the agency of workers to better achieve their desired outcomes. CHAT concepts are deliberately deployed within Change Laboratory as cultural tools.

Change Laboratories are typically a series of workshops of around two hours at a time. There is no fixed number or schedule for implementing Change Laboratories in a workplace, but in the case of Haneul Early Learning Center (Chapter 7), they were held at roughly monthly intervals across a six-month period. Change Laboratories are typically facilitated by

a team of researchers who collaborate with the other Laboratory participants to develop new conceptual and practical tools in response to workplace contradictions and the conflicting motives that result. The aim is to
resolve these barriers to achievement of workplace objects by designing and
trialing new forms of practice. In the research project involving Haneul
Early Learning Center, pairs of leaders (typically the center's Director plus
one other senior staff member) were recruited from ten long-day childcare
services and provided their consent for their participation to be documented as research data. The Change Laboratories with the twenty participants
were facilitated by me and a Research Assistant, who audio recorded and
transcribed the workshops as well as making in vivo fieldnotes.

The first workshop began by exploring and clarifying, with the leaders,
the objects of their workplace activity and the outcomes at which these
objects are directed. These outcomes are typically broad; in an early
childhood center, for example, the outcome might be articulated as
providing high-quality education and care to children and families.
Motivating objects of activity are more discrete and are often task-oriented;
in the case of an early childhood center these can include "assessing and
reporting children's learning," "implementing daily routines," and "involving parents in their children's learning." Fulfillment of these objects of
activity relies on coherent, rather than contradictory, alignment of rules,
tools, and divisions of labor in the workplace system.

Change Laboratories are supplemented by gathering preliminary data to
try to understand some contemporary features of practice in the workplace
and the history of how these have developed. These data may be interviews
with the workers about the workplace and what they are trying to achieve
(the approach used with Haneul's leaders and their colleagues), or direct
observation of work practices, which may be videotaped and replayed in
the workshops. These data are then analyzed by the researchers with
several purposes in mind. First, they help the participants in the Change
Laboratories (both workers and researchers) understand the history of
specific workplace objects, including previous attempts to resolve problems
of practice. Second, the researchers look carefully for evidence of contradictions, which appear as conflicts of motives within systems of workplace
activity, resulting in obstacles to fulfillment of objects of activity. Third,
during the Change Laboratories the researchers "mirror" elements of this
previous data back to the workers to bring contradictions into conscious
view. These "mirror data" provide a first stimulus from which workers and
researchers can work together to explore possibilities for new workplace
practices. Once new practices have been conceptualized, they are

implemented by the workers and reviewed in subsequent Change Laboratories, including grappling with new contradictions that arise as plans for change are implemented. Documentation of the Change Laboratories, through methods such as fieldnotes and videorecording, records participants' accounts of change in their workplace(s) as well as providing ongoing mirror data.

Double stimulation is at the core of Change Laboratory methodology. Practical problems in the workplace provide the first stimulus. The second stimulus takes the form of tools and/or signs that can be used to remediate practice by addressing the contradictions underpinning the first stimulus. These tools or signs may be contributed by the researchers or the workplace participants, can be an adaptation of existing workplace tools, or can be designed by participants together within or between the Change Laboratories. In other words, the second stimuli offered to participants in the Change Laboratories alongside the first stimulus can take a variety of forms, depending on the problem of practice under consideration. However, one tool is typically offered: the conceptual model that supports them to analyze the workplace activity system (Figure 6.1). The researcher-facilitator of the Change Laboratories can use this tool analytically and also, more importantly, show the other participants how to use this tool to analyze the current conditions of their work. This model allows Change Laboratory participants to examine past and present practices by mobilizing the concepts of tools, rules, community, subject, division of labor, and objects of activity. Workers and researchers can then use the tool to collaboratively identify contradictions within and between workplace norms and artifacts in a systematic way and bring these to conscious awareness.

In some cases, the participants may also use the model to understand how activity systems interact with neighboring systems. For example, a kindergarten and a nearby school operate as separate systems of activity, but the cultural norms of one system can have frustrating implications for the other system, particularly at the point when children make the transition from kindergarten to school. The extensive research that has been carried out in relation to transition to school (see Boyle et al., 2018) is evidence of ongoing attempts to identify and resolve the contradictions between preschool and school education that play out as conflicting motives for children, families, and professionals.

Early childhood services, like any workplace system, are dense with contradictions. This is not to imply these workplaces are necessarily riven with negative conflict or problematic dilemmas; rather, contradictions are a positive outgrowth of human activity that offer the possibility of development and change. Many contradictions are not new but have accumulated historically, sometimes over many decades. Engeström (1993) uses the concept of *sedimentation* to describe forms of practice that have been laid down over a long period of time and which contain the traces of earlier practices. Sedimented forms of practice cease to be consciously examined and can simply become *how we do things around here*. Latent or just-emerging opportunities to develop practices are characterized by Engeström as "buds or shoots" (p. 68) of possible futures. Despite the occurrence of "buds" signaling new opportunities for practice, humans retain a remarkable capacity to live with contradictions over long periods of time.

A key role of the researcher in Change Laboratories is to question sedimented practices so that they are exposed to critique. As Ellis (2011) argues, "The goal of a post-Marxist historical analysis, therefore, is to reveal the conditions under which the origins of social practices came to be routinised or sedimented and the possible system of alternatives concealed" (p. 191); the work of Change Laboratories is to open up these alternatives by "reactivating consciousness of the historically contingent changes in activity systems" (Ellis, 2011, p. 191). This reactivation brings examination of systems into the present and stimulates workers to imagine possible futures, or generate what Sannino and Engeström (2017, p. 81) call "possibility knowledge." Miettinen (2013) has argued this can be a profoundly creative form of intervention. In part, this is because there is no expectation that the researchers will provide the answers to problems of practice. The researchers can offer tools and ask searching questions but, ultimately, the intervention relies on the agency of the workers who are the experts in the practices they are examining. Within Change Laboratory methodology, the workplace participants have the primary responsibility for analyzing past and present practice, and for imagining and enacting future practices.

A critical element in identifying successful change is that the new practices provide evidence of "expansion" of objects of activity. This expansion is evidenced by deeper and more complex understandings about practice, and practices that more fully meet the objects of activity – and, ultimately, the desired outcomes – that motivate workers' shared labor processes. Changes can also extend beyond expansion of objects of activity to reconstruct multiple aspects of the workplace system, including rules, tools, divisions of labor, and even outcomes. Engeström and Sannino (2010) use the term *expansive learning* to denote the way in which working through a conflict of motives not only deepens understanding of workplace objects of activity but leads to change at the level of workplace systems. Such system-level development can be conceptualized within the Vygotskian tradition as movement within a *collective* zone of proximal development.

It is worth nothing that Change Laboratory methodology is not without its critics. One persistent criticism of the Change Laboratory approach is that has been coopted by the interests of capital to increase efficiency in health, education, and business workplaces with an accompanying "apparent occlusion of broader social relations" (Levant, 2018, p. 103). Levant cites Avis (2007), Warmington (2008), and Bakhurst (2009), who have all challenged the neglect of class as a central category in a Marxian analysis. Warmington (2008) summarizes this critique by arguing "his [Engeström's] historical accumulation [of contradictions] appears to be located in the site of local, technical practices, rather than in the contradictions inherent in social class relations" (p. 10). Sannino and Engeström (2017) have offered a partial response to this critique by pointing out that Change Laboratory seeks to be generative, rather than generalizable; in other words, implications for wider theory and practice (such as raising consciousness of class relations) can be validly generated out of local cases (see also Becker, 2014). At the same time, Engeström and Sannino's scholarship is increasingly concerned with marginalized people, including recovering drug addicts (Sannino, 2022) and inhabitants of Brazilian favelas (Ferreira Lemos & Engeström, 2018).

This claim to consciousness-raising, anchored in Marxian understandings of alienation and agency, is enacted in Change Laboratory through two main theoretical principles that offer a link between transformation of local work practices and wider systemic oppression: *ascension from the abstract to the concrete* and *transformative agency*.

6.7 From Abstraction to (Re)Concretization

One of the most well-known quotes from Marx's published work (and also inscribed on his grave in London's Highgate Cemetery) is "The philosophers have only interpreted the world, in various ways. The point, however, is to change it" (Marx, 1845, p. 15). This statement encapsulates the abiding concern of Marxian thought: to not simply conceptualize the world in more complex and abstracted ways, but to use those concepts to transform the everyday conditions of people in the world. In our view, this concern has particular salience for the work of leaders in education settings.

Much research and analysis in the social sciences seeks to build or test theories to better understand workplace phenomena. This scholarly work is valuable and important. Its major limitation for practitioners, though, is that it does not point to how their concrete problems of practice might be *reconcretized* as new forms of practice. However, the process of generating abstract insights out of practical problems, then using those insights to general new practical solutions is one of the key principles of the Change Laboratory process. Chapter 7 describes the case example of how this was achieved by the leadership team at Haneul Early Learning Center. In brief, by examining the concrete realities of present practice, recasting these realities in abstract form through the use of concepts such as "division of labor," and using the resulting analysis to design and test newly concretized practices, the center's leaders were able to resolve a persistent problem of staffing practice that had wide implications for the quality of colleagues', children's, and families' experiences of life in the center.

6.8   Transformative Agency

A third principle underpinning Change Laboratory methodology, along with double stimulation and reconcretization of practice, is *transformative agency*. Sannino (2015) describes transformative agency as "extending agency beyond the skin of the individual toward collective transformative endeavors"; these endeavors she identifies as "volitional actions that transform the world we inhabit." (p. 1). Transformative agency is fostered by Change Laboratories because:

> This type of intervention carries future-oriented visions loaded with initiative and commitment. Such visions materialize in novel concepts and practices that enable collaborative development beyond authoritative organizational constraints. Societally impactful knowledge is actionable knowledge, that is, knowledge that can be turned into transformative action. We suggest that actionable knowledge is typically *possibility knowledge* (Engeström, 2007), in other words, knowledge about what might be possible new forms and patterns of objects and phenomena in our life worlds and social institutions. (Sannino & Engeström, 2017, p 81, italics in original)

In summary, Change Laboratories employ the process of double stimulation to provoke this "possibility knowledge" that can then be reconcretized in new or revised practices. Because these changes are understood dialectically (not as teleological moves from internal mind to external practice, or from individual will to collective effort), individual minds change *at the same time* as collective practice changes. These shifts are frequently (although not always) characterized by an increased sense of agency among individuals and teams, evident as increased capacity not only to imagine future practices but to test and reflect on their implementation. This was indeed the case at Haneul Early Learning Center.

6.9   Conclusion

This chapter has provided the briefest of introductions to key concepts in CHAT. For readers interested in pursuing the underpinnings of CHAT further, concepts such as agency, germ cell, and boundary crossing also bear investigation, in addition to developing a deeper understanding of key concepts already touched on in this chapter. For the purposes of this book, these CHAT concepts underpin Change Laboratory methodology as an intervention in workplace practices and serve as explanatory and analytic tools for researching and understanding those practices.

In Chapter 7, the example of Haneul Early Learning Center is followed step-by-step through a sequence of Change Laboratories to show how these concepts can be applied to the development of leaders in early childhood education settings. As the present chapter has argued, Change Laboratory is anchored in a history of ideas that positions it as more than an instrumental or technical intervention, and this is especially the case in settings where the labor power contributed by workers is greater than the exchange value they receive in the form of wages. This remains the case in many early childhood education settings in Australia and elsewhere. Approaches to leadership development that grapple with the deep contradictions underpinning early childhood education provision in contemporary society continue, therefore, to be essential.

CHAPTER 7

Leading Organizational Change: The Case of Haneul Early Learning Center

Joce

This chapter provides a narrative case example of a formative intervention in early childhood education leadership practice using the principles and practices of Change Laboratory outlined in Chapter 6. The case is of Haneul Early Learning Center (this name is a pseudonym), specifically the two teachers responsible for leading the development of curriculum and pedagogy in the center. The chapter draws on research data generated at five time points during the intervention to illustrate the use of Change Laboratory as a methodology for practice development, particularly for workplace leaders, and how this methodology is underpinned by concepts from cultural-historical activity theory (CHAT).

The chapter begins with a description of the research and development site for the case study – Haneul Early Learning Center – and two of its leaders, Elsa and Rebecca (also pseudonyms). It then draws on an initial interview with Elsa and Rebecca to describe professional practice in the center at the beginning of the intervention. Elsa and Rebecca were two of a group of twenty-four center leaders (recruited, in pairs, from twelve Melbourne early learning centers) who, in 2019, participated in a series of Change Laboratories designed to equip them with new cultural tools to develop their practices of leadership. Elsa and Rebecca's work across a series of six Change Laboratories involved the development of a new process for staff induction at Haneul Early Learning Center. The shifting motives and development of new rules, tools, and divisions of labor involved in this work are described in the main part of this chapter, but only briefly. The main purpose of the chapter is to illustrate how a shift in Elsa and Rebecca's leadership capacity changed between the beginning and the end of the intervention. The case of Elsa and Rebecca is particular to Haneul Early Learning Center, but is presented here as a vehicle for elaborating and reconcretizing concepts from CHAT as they play out in a series of Change Laboratories and at the worksites of participants. Thus, the final part of the chapter focuses on the outcomes of the intervention for

Elsa, Rebecca, and their center, and connects shifts in practice to principles derived from CHAT and related practices within the Change Laboratories.

7.1 The Narrative Case

The unit of analysis when researching and mobilizing Change Laboratory interventions is the activity *system* of the workplace itself, which provides the site for understanding a "case" of practice development. As explained in Chapter 6, activity systems are complex and dynamic assemblages of subjects, rules, tools, community, and divisions of labor that are more or less aligned with the achievement of a motivating object of activity that, in turn, fulfills the desired outcomes of the workplace. In an early learning center, this desired outcome is typically expressed along the lines of "high-quality education and care for all children" and this was indeed the case for Haneul Early Learning Center.

7.1.1 The Activity System: Haneul Early Learning Center

Haneul Early Learning Center is located in the city center in Melbourne, Australia. Parents and caregivers who enrol their children in the center are mainly office workers or work in nearby service settings, such as cafés. The center is licensed to care for up to ninety children at any one time across five classrooms, including up to twenty-four infants (children under the age of two years). At the time that Elsa and Rebecca joined the leadership project there were around thirty-five staff regularly employed in the center; this large number of staff in relation to ninety children is attributable to the fact that very few of these staff were working full-time in the center. The stability of staff employment was a particular issue for the center, and it provides an underpinning theme for the practice changes described in this chapter. Elsa and Rebecca had both joined the center within the past two years and, in the months prior to their employment, the center had experienced a 70% turnover in staffing.

7.1.2 The Change Laboratory Participants: Elsa and Rebecca

Elsa had joined the center as a full-time kindergarten teacher (leading the program for four-year-old children in their year prior to school entry). This position included designation as the center's "Educational Leader." This is a mandatory position in Australian early childhood services, charged with leading the ongoing development of curriculum and pedagogy; in this sense, the position contrasts with longer-standing conceptualizations of leadership in early childhood services, which have tended to focus on center administration and management (Whalley, 2011). Rebecca was employed a few months after Elsa, in the position of 2IC (Deputy Director or "second-in-charge") for administration and management. Rebecca's position also included responsibility for sharing Elsa's designated Educational Leader position.

Both Elsa and Rebecca were highly experienced early childhood teachers, each with more than ten years in teaching and leadership positions, and both hold bachelor's degrees in early childhood education. Perhaps inevitably, then, issues related to staff qualifications arose in their first interview, which I have designated *Time 1* in this case study.

7.2 Time 1: Haneul Early Learning Center – Before the Change Laboratory Intervention

The purpose of gathering data before beginning a series of Change Laboratories is twofold. First, it allows the researcher-participants to gain an overall sense of the workplace and some of its current practice problems, as identified by the workplace participants. Second, these practice problems can be analyzed for their underpinning contradictions, and the history of how these contradictions arose, then "mirrored" back to the participants at the first Change Laboratory. These "mirror data" are both a stimulus to discussion in the Change Laboratories and a way in which the researcher-participants can test, with the workplace participants, the resonance and salience of the researchers' initial analysis of the activity system. As the formative intervention proceeds, data generated during each Change Laboratory can also be presented as mirror data in subsequent Change Laboratories.

In the initial joint interview with Elsa and Rebecca, they began by describing the "messy" way they had found themselves in their leadership roles at Haneul Early Learning Center:

> Right, it was actually very messy. I arrived here at Haneul while it was in a lot of turbulence and the [Educational Leader] role sat with the Director and then, when I arrived, it sat with another person on our staff who was quite overwhelmed by the role. I was asked to sit in at a meeting and then I was given the role. Which I wasn't unhappy about, I was ready for a challenge, so to speak. Then, when Rebecca's job was advertised and Rebecca was successful, they labeled that role as Educational Leader, which has not changed to 2IC. So, it was quite a messy entry into the role and it

was my first go at Educational Leader, I guess. However, it seems we have navigated through the storm and here we are. (Elsa, interview 1, lines 14–21)

For Rebecca, her entry into the Educational Leader role, just described by Elsa, was something of a surprise:

REBECCA: When I started here, I applied for this role as the 2IC, not knowing that there was a second role of the Ed Leader until I actually started on my first day.

INTERVIEWER: And then what happened?

REBECCA: It was just, I don't know how it happened, it was just a bit messy, [the] paperwork was messy and, like Elsa has said previously, it was a time where things weren't happening too well here at Haneul. So, then I rolled with that and then Elsa was Ed Leader as well. I learned that throughout my, I think, first two days of being here and I was, like, let's roll with it. I'm not going to push Elsa aside, I'm actually going to work alongside her. . . . We just clicked, absolutely clicked, and we've been like that since.
(Rebecca, interview 1, lines 41–52)

At the time Elsa and Rebecca were interviewed, this experience of serendipitous leadership was not uncommon in early childhood education, resulting in what Coleman et al. (2016) have called "accidental leaders."

It is fortunate that Elsa and Rebecca were strongly aligned in their approach to professional practice – "clicked" was Rebecca's term – as they immediately encountered the center's problem of unstable staff employment practices.

ELSA: If I was being honestly honest . . . it was quite horrible. It was very, very, horrible.

REBECCA: I think for me, yeah, I was absolutely processing, like, just, what's happening, who's who, what do I do, who do I answer to, basically.

INTERVIEWER: Sure.

REBECCA: What do I need to provide the staff with, where are the staff.

ELSA: Who are our actual staff members and who are agency [casual hire] staff members. That was a big thing for a long time.
(Elsa and Rebecca, interview 1, lines 121–130)

In CHAT terms, Elsa and Rebecca's initial problem was fundamental:

• Who is the *subject* of the workplace activity system?

This subject – the center staff – takes collective form, includes Elsa and Rebecca themselves, and is the agent that takes volitional action (Sannino, 2015) to develop and perpetuate the workplace activity system. In addition to trying to work out who comprised the staff group, Elsa and Rebecca were facing incursions from an adjacent activity system – the state Department of Education responsible for regulating early childhood services.

ELSA: I was so relieved when Rebecca arrived because it was quite a horrible couple of months. We had the Department here all the time and 24 points of non-compliance [with national Regulations] . . . It was very distressing and, even though I had no capacity to leave my classroom, it seemingly fell on our shoulders when all these noncompliances continued to happen. You know [for example], "Oh, these teachers still don't understand the planning cycle. What are you doing about it?"

(Elsa, interview 1, lines 158–164)

To complicate matters, Elsa and Rebecca also faced the problem of finding time when the two of them could meet to discuss how they would respond to the demands being made on their joint Educational Leader role:

ELSA: [I'm] still full time in the [kindergarten] room and, I guess, Rebecca and I often, well, we make time . . . I love teaching, but I have a very special. . . – I love being in the Educational Leadership role. So we seem to make time for it, even though all our other jobs, like all the 2IC stuff which Rebecca has to do . . . Yesterday it was "Oh yeah, we've got to talk about Educational Leadership stuff," and then we started talking and we were, like, "Let's have a meeting quickly now."

INTERVIEWER: So where were you when you were having that conversation, are you in your [class]room?

ELSA: No, we were in the office. Actually, it was my lunch break.

(Elsa, interview 1, lines 169–180)

Rebecca also described being caught between the two parts of her position – 2IC and Educational Leader:

REBECCA: Yeah, I think being 2IC and sharing that Ed Leadership role is already a struggle and it's an ongoing struggle. I think if I didn't have Elsa supporting me in the Ed Leader role as well, as we support each other, there was just no way one person can do it.

INTERVIEWER: Why is it a struggle? What makes it a struggle, Rebecca?

REBECCA: I think, for me, because of the management role that I have and where I need to step in. Like, for example, right now I've got to be in the center Director role for about a month because my Director's on leave, which means that I put Ed Leader stuff on the back side.

(Rebecca, interview 1, lines 197–204)

Rebecca went on to explain that this tension arose from the two roles having "different expectations." Elsa then elaborated on this point, explaining that these different expectations related not only to managerial versus pedagogical tasks, but to how staff had repositioned the Educational Leader as a "management" role:

ELSA: It gets a bit blurry for me sometimes when I have to teach, obviously, with my team, and I'm just a teacher alongside all the other teachers . . . [but] . . . sometimes I'm not asked or I'm just not privy or people find it uncomfortable. I don't often hear a lot of the whisperings that go on any more. There's this line and they will often say, "But you're management." I'm not, I'm truly not.

(Elsa, interview 1, lines 238–242)

By this stage in the interview, it was clear that the activity system at Haneul Early Learning Center was experiencing multiple contradictions in relation to the *division of labor*. These included a contradiction between the *rule* that the Educational Leader would meet high expectations, and the *division of labor* that distributed the role across two people without providing time for them to consult with each other. This division of labor was further complicated by the expectation that Elsa would take up part of the Educational Leader role while also maintaining her full-time teaching role in the kindergarten classroom, and that Rebecca would be both part-Educational Leader and second-in-charge of center management. This approach to the division of labor meant that both Elsa and Rebecca experienced a continuous and contradictory "double bind" between the motives of each role. This was particularly the case for Rebecca. Figure 7.1 summarizes the tensions between the developmental expectations placed on the Educational Leader, and the management and compliance expectations on a center Director.

A second contradictory aspect of the activity system that was described by Elsa and Rebecca was the relationship between staff qualifications (a characteristic of the *subjects* of the activity system) and high-quality curriculum and pedagogy (*objects of the activity system*). This was touched on when Elsa referred to the requirement from the Department of Education to improve the center's approach to planning for children's learning. Later in the interview, Rebecca referred to this problem when asked what they would like to focus on during the intervention project:

REBECCA: One of the main projects that we want to sort of roll out is educating the other team members that are not on the leadership team or the management or don't have another role besides teaching. Sort of upskilling them and having them out and about and hearing what the new research is saying, basically.

(Rebecca, interview 1, lines 294–298)

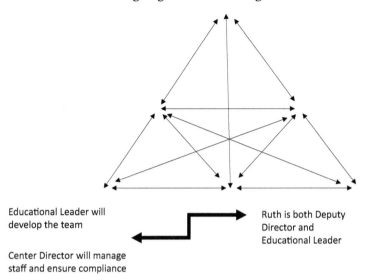

Figure 7.1   Tension between rules (norms of behavior) and division of labor.

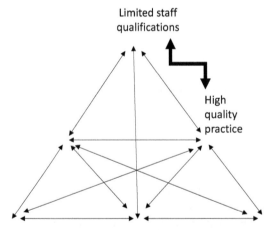

Figure 7.2   Tension between object of high-quality practice and limited conceptual tools available to staff due to qualification levels.

When asked about the center's qualifications profile, Elsa explained that roughly one-third of center staff had only a sub-Diploma qualification, which she categorized as "unqualified." The variability of qualifications across the early childhood sector is a persistent problem in Australia that results in the contradiction portrayed in Figure 7.2.

Elsa and Rebecca's strategy to address this lack of knowledge was to conceptualize development "projects" for individual staff members:

INTERVIEWER: What kind of things [projects]?

ELSA: [We] try and look at individuals, don't we [*looking at Rebecca*], and try to look at where people are at and where there might be needs ... So what we've been working on right now is thinking about our individual team members, and we've got quite a lot of new team members, [understanding] where everyone is at, and to know where are some people's passions. We're finding our new teacher is really invested in the drama space and wants to use the studio for craft. Great, so how are we supporting her? But one thing we were hoping to have already [is] a bit of a passport for each of our teachers to really showcase where they've been, where they're going.

INTERVIEWER: Showcase to whom?

ELSA: Showcase to one another, you know, "Hey, I'm a big one for this [practice]," [alongside another staff member who is thinking] "Oh, you know, I'm really struggling, for example, at the moment with what really embedded Indigenous practice looks like in the classroom ..."

(Elsa, interview 1, lines 398–416)

This focus on development at the individual level (both to showcase strengths and to influence colleagues' practices) has been one of the most persistent features of pre-Change Laboratory interviews with Educational Leaders across several years of our research program into leadership development in early childhood education. It is closely akin to the goals of individual development also set by Elsa and Rebecca for themselves as leaders. Elsa said, "I think I'd like to carry on, I guess, for my own, kind of, personal knowledge, continue to work on what it looks like to be an effective leader and a classroom teacher." While this individualized approach is understandable, given the dominant discourses of individual development in both education and educational psychology across the past century, in workplace settings like Haneul Early Learning Center, with its high turnover of staff, practice change can prove elusive unless development is conceptualized and enacted at the *systemic* level. I return to this point later in the chapter, as I describe the changes Elsa and Rebecca fostered in their center, beginning with their goals identified at Time 2 – the first Change Laboratory.

7.3 Time 2: Change Laboratory 1 – Identifying Contradictions

The pre-Change Laboratory interviews with participants typically prime them to reflect on the practice problems they want to resolve during the formative intervention. By the time they reached Change Laboratory 1,

Elsa and Rebecca had identified an issue that was pressing because it was posing a risk to children's safety in the center.

Because of the center's inner-city location, outdoor play space for the children was limited, so outdoor play times were rostered across the five classrooms to keep different age groups separate during play. The rationale for this was that it was a way of ensuring that older children would not accidently harm younger children during active play times. This was an aspect of center practice that had been developed in the distant past, through a process of *explicit mediation* that had established the rules (which classroom could use the outdoor space at what times) and division of labor (which teachers would be responsible for supervision of indoor and outdoor play). However, this complex practice had become *implicit* in the center, a part of "how we do things around here," and therefore not always explicitly addressed when new staff were engaged. This resulted in the contradictory scenario summarized in Figure 7.3.

Elsa and Rebecca therefore resolved that their focus for the formative intervention would be on improving the safety of children's outdoor play.

However, between Change Laboratory 1 and Change Laboratory 2, workplace participants are asked to take a closer look at practices in their workplaces, both the practice selected for development and other practices in general. The concept of contradiction, introduced to the workplace participants in Change Laboratory 1, is central to this exercise:

• What practices do participants identify that are in contradiction with other practices?

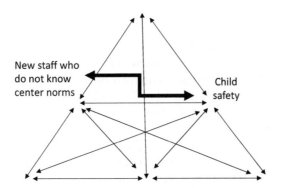

Figure 7.3   Contradiction between object of child safety and subjects who have not yet internalized center rules and expectations.

- Where a particular practice is problematic, what aspects of center norms (i.e., rules, tools, divisions of labor, also introduced in the first Change Laboratory) are contradicting each other to hinder the effectiveness of the practice?
- What is the history of attempts to resolve some of these contradictions? And why did these attempts not succeed?

Like many Change Laboratory participants, Elsa and Rebecca were able to identify a large number of contradictions in their workplace system. This is neither unusual – workplaces are almost always complex and contradictory systems – nor is this necessarily problematic, since contradictions are the essential starting points for practice development. In the second Change Laboratory, the participants collectively explored these contradictions and related practices, sometimes leading to identification of even deeper contradictions.

7.4 Time 3: Change Laboratory 2 – A Shift in the Motive Object of Activity

For Elsa and Rebecca, this period of observation resulted in an awareness of a deeper contradiction that was leading to difficulties with outdoor play. Having observed the complexities of the outside play routines and spoken with colleagues about the center's norms around outside play, they noticed that disruptions to outside play most commonly occurred when newly appointed casual or ongoing staff were involved. Elsa and Rebecca realized that the norms guiding the use of the outdoor play space had become implicit (as noted in Section 7.3) and were not routinely being made explicit to new staff. As they discussed this insight with their current colleagues, they heard multiple accounts of poor enculturation into the center's norms from recently appointed staff across multiple aspects of practice. At the same time, longer-term staff shared many examples of how their work had been interrupted and their time taken up in explaining the center's rules and divisions of labor (in CHAT terms) to new staff, not only in relation to outdoor play but a whole range of day-to-day practices.

Their analysis of these accounts led Elsa and Rebecca to believe that a more effective system of induction for new staff members could address multiple *objects of activity* related to center staffing. These included not only "reducing interruptions for existing staff" and "increasing safety for children during outside play," but "reducing frustration for new staff," since these frustrations were possibly contributing to high staff turnover.

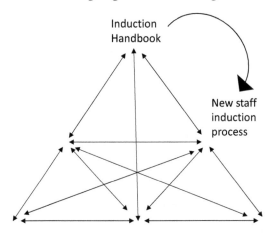

Figure 7.4   Development of a new Induction Handbook becomes a temporary object of activity to resolve multiple contradictions.

By the end of the second Change Laboratory, Elsa and Rebecca had identified an additional motive object of activity among their *hierarchy of motives* for their leadership practice, as shown in Figure 7.4.

7.5   Time 4: Change Laboratory 3 – Collective Design of New Practices

One of the important features of Change Laboratory is that it mobilizes processes of *collaborative creativity* to design new practices. For Elsa and Rebecca, this meant that they did not shoulder the burden of designing (then unilaterally imposing) a new induction program at Haneul Early Learning Center; rather, having initially explored current practice problems with their colleagues, they then presented the contradiction summarized in Figure 7.3 to their colleagues and explored everyone's suggestions about how this contradiction might be resolved through a deeper analysis of practices of staff induction.

In this way, a contradiction that is hampering practice becomes a focus for practice development in the early stages of the *expansive learning cycle*. In other words, the *idea* of a new induction program became an *object* for *expansion* by the staff team, including development of new *rules* ("the new program must be cost effective"), new *divisions of labor* ("new staff will spend a week observing practice and asking questions across all the classrooms before they begin teaching"), and new *cultural tools* to *mediate* activity. The main cultural tool was an Induction Handbook, initially drafted by Elsa and Rebecca, then shared with the whole team for feedback and amendment. In this phase of the *expansive learning cycle* at Haneul Early Learning Center, the Induction Handbook became a *common object* of psychological activity for everyone on the team. Serendipitously, a new senior staff member joined the teaching team during the formative intervention, so Elsa, Rebecca, and their colleagues were able to trial and get feedback on their new system of staff induction, including the Handbook, in real time.

7.6 Time 5: Postintervention – Consolidation of New Practices

Each of the leadership pairs involved in the project was interviewed within the weeks following the final Change Laboratory. These interviews provided not only an opportunity to reflect on and celebrate success with practice changes, but an empirical touchpoint regarding the operationalization of CHAT concepts. I return here, and in the concluding section in this chapter, to the concepts introduced in Chapter 6 to show how they were evident in Elsa and Rebecca's conscious understanding at the end of the formative intervention in their leadership practice.

7.6.1 Internalization and Externalization

The first concepts often evident in postintervention interviews are *internalization* and *externalization*, which are seen when interviewees describe how they have absorbed the activity system model introduced in the Change Laboratories as a new *cultural tool* and put it to practical use. Elsa described the nature of this internal/external dialectic when she said,

ELSA: We've just gone through an overview and reflection of the Educational Leadership function within [their governing body] . . . And this tool is just at the forefront of your mind. I could barely even think about all the other things that we covered this year, because this is the thing that I'd like to keep moving forward with. So, I think in terms of being able to now lead next steps with our team, and I know we literally said, "Triangles everywhere!"

(Elsa, interview 2, lines 58–63)

Here Elsa is describing a process of reflection and recall, as well as a process of thinking forward with the tool in mind. In this way, the tool (the triangular model of an activity system) provides an auxiliary stimulus (or "second stimulus") in relation to the first stimulus (the practice problem), thereby facilitating the process of *double stimulation*.

> The word "double" in the principle of double stimulation refers to two types of stimuli that interact to induce agency. The first stimulus is a challenging situation, e.g., the problematic activity itself. It manifests itself as problems, disturbances, ruptures, and contradictions that convey to the practitioners that there is a need to change their activity in one way or another. The second stimulus consists usually of instrumental artifacts (such as models produced during the intervention described in this article) given to or constructed by the subject to serve as instruments that help to break away from the problematic situation (Sannino, 2015). In other words, such instrumental artifacts, or auxiliary stimuli, form the basis of the process of building transformative agency. According to Engeström and Sannino (2013), the breaking away from the original problematic situation using the second stimulus proceeds in two steps: (i) an artifact, or an auxiliary stimulus, is chosen or created and loaded with meaning and sense, (ii) an action is laid out using the artifact as a mediator sign that allows the subject to control actions and understand the problem or the initial circumstances (Vänninen et al., 2021, pp. 2–3).

Rebecca went on to describe one way she thought the tool could help change and reconcretize external practices.

REBECCA: It's great that management – and a few of us Ed Leaders in the organization – actually have had the opportunity to participate in the project. But I think it will make teachers more effective in relation to reflecting on practices and documentation and all sorts that teachers carry.
(Rebecca, interview 2, lines 84–88)

7.6.2 Mediation by Cultural Tools

Elsa's suggestion that the tool can "make" teachers think in different ways relates to its *mediating* function. When Elsa says, "You can really picture it in your mind and see, 'Oh, okay. So that's sitting up there. These are the kind of tools that we're working with. And this is the outcome that we'd like" (Elsa, interview 2, lines 93–95), she is explaining how the triangular model of the activity system (see Chapter 6, Figure 6.1) appears to her (internal) "mind's eye" as *mediational means* for thinking about (external) desired practices.

This reconceptualization of *cultural tools* and the *remediation* of practice made possible through this process can be generalized to other tools, signs, and resources that mediate practice. For example, Elsa and Rebecca had developed new meanings in relation to *time* as a cultural tool that is available to their practices of Educational Leadership. Having described (in the preintervention interview) their struggle to find time for the role, noted in Section 7.2, in the postintervention interview their perspective on time had shifted.

INTERVIEWER: [In the first interview] you mentioned the fact that you were going through a little bit of an upheaval during –
ELSA: Yeah, yeah, that's right. And there are always going to be things, though. But I think this is an important aspect of practice. So, I think any practice change is going to be quite the journey. And to invest in a tool that we could see from the outset that it was probably going to work, means that we wanted to make the time, so I'm not really [time] limited.
REBECCA: No, not at all.

(Elsa and Rebecca, interview 2, lines 435–441)

Elsa and Rebecca were still finding it challenging to make time for the Educational Leader role, but the *meaning* attributed to their time use had changed because they could see that their plans made using the triangular model of their activity system were "probably going to work."

7.6.3   Collective Creativity in Working on Shared Motive Objects of Activity

There were two notable features of the way Elsa and Rebecca took up the tools offered in the Change Laboratories (particularly the model of the *activity system* and the cycle of *expansive learning*) with their colleagues. The first was the way they used these tools to both foster and reflect on *collective creativity* across their team in relation to solving problems of practice.

In the preintervention interview, Elsa and Rebecca described a conceptualization of practice change where (i) the individual teacher was the unit of analysis for practice change, but (ii) the Educational Leaders were responsible for imagining and implementing strategies to develop practice. Elsa and Rebecca's implementation of the expansive learning cycle in their center overturned these individualized and hierarchical norms of practice at Haneul Early Learning Center. By provoking their colleagues to treat induction of new staff as a shared or *common* object of activity that, if and when expanded, could overcome multiple risks and irritants for teachers and children, Elsa and Rebecca were relieved of the burden of having to have all the answers to problems of practice and therefore taking responsibility for whether practice changes succeeded or failed. Design of the new approach to staff induction was a process of *collective creativity*.

7.6.4   *Temporary Objects of Activity*

The second feature of the way Elsa and Rebecca used the Change Laboratory tools was to radically alter the center's *division of labor* around responsibility for solving problems of practice. Multiple objects were examined and negotiated by the team at Haneul Early Learning Center under Elsa and Rebecca's leadership, but the most crucial of these in relation to the staff induction project was the center's *division of labor*. Elsa and Rebecca made the division of labor around staff induction a *temporary object of activity*. By becoming both a *temporary* and a *common* object, the center's division of labor could be subjected to *expansion*. In other words, as the team engaged with this shared object, they deepened and enriched their understandings of how work was (and could be) carried out in the center. Multiple aspects of this temporary object had to be negotiated, including:

- Who will undertake the teaching role of the new staff member while they spend their first week in the center observing and asking questions?
- Whose role is it to answer the new staff member's questions?
- What is the new staff member expected to do during their week of induction?
- How and when will new staff have opportunities to contribute new ideas and critique what they have observed at Haneul Early Learning Center?

As these questions were explored, questions about other aspects of the activity system inevitably arose. Many questions were related to other cultural tools and resources, such as money, time, and materials:

- How will the center fund the additional staff member needed when the new staff member is being inducted?
- What will the center ensure time is set aside for discussion and reflection with new colleagues?
- What adjustments need to be made to center policies to reflect and govern these new practices?
- What changes will need to be made to the staff roster?
- What printed materials need to be developed? And when, how, and to whom will these be distributed?

These questions are by no means an exhaustive list of the issues the team at Haneul Early Learning Center needed to explore to develop new practices of staff induction. The salient point in the context of this chapter, however, is that this work was a *shared* exploration undertaken around a *common concern*. Elsa and Rebecca reported that this process not only resulted in a sense of shared ownership of the new practices but an increased sense that, with respect to designing new practices in the future, "We can go for it!" (Elsa, interview 2, line 123).

Many of the principles of Change Laboratory were evident in the final interview with Elsa and Rebecca, including internalization, externalization, mediation, double stimulation, collective creativity, motive objects of activity, and common motives. The concluding part of this chapter builds on these principles to explain how they come together to offer a way forward for leadership development methodologies in early childhood education.

7.7 Conclusion: Why Was the Change Laboratory Intervention at Haneul Early Learning Center Effective?

The theoretical principles of Change Laboratory are necessary but not sufficient to explain the success of the formative intervention conducted with Elsa and Rebecca, and which they in turn conducted with their colleagues. In this final section, we turn to some of the deeper understandings about work and working life that we believe need to be borne in mind when thinking about how formative interventions can enable leadership in early childhood settings.

7.7.1 Effective Leaders Understand Work as a Social and Emotional Phenomenon

It is worth pausing to contrast Elsa and Rebecca's enthusiasm at the prospect of inducting new staff in the future with their earlier dismay at their experience of staff turnover. We suggest his shift in tone can be attributed to the *social and emotional investment* workers have in their work.

ELSA: We're really invested, I think. Which is a big thing too, because it's the investment of everyone. You know, what do we want our team to be like? This? We want strong pedagogical induction to the Haneul team. And I think most of our team now could actually say, "Yes, this is what we want from you [as Educational Leaders] when you're coming in. And this is what our role is. And this is what [Rebecca's] role is. And my role is." And kind of, that distribution of leadership and skills and all those sorts of things.
(Elsa, interview 2, lines 99–104)

We understand Elsa's renewed emotional engagement in her work to be, at least in part, due to her increased clarity around the *motive objects of activity* of her work as Educational Leader, including providing "strong pedagogical induction."

7.7.2 *Effective Leadership Enhances Agency*

Increased emotional engagement is frequently accompanied by greater feelings of agency for workers. Through a facilitated process of *double stimulation* that brings new tools (the second stimulus) to existing problems of practice (the first stimulus), Change Laboratory participants learn to act, rather than react.

ELSA: I reckon we could give most things a crack these days. And, actually, give them a really good go ... When we arrived here and we tried to get things like action research off the ground, it was dead. It was absolutely dead. We went nowhere. We literally went nowhere. But these days, it's actually great. It's actually great saying that.

(Elsa, interview 2, lines 134–138)

Here Elsa is talking about practices within the center, but she also gave an example of agency in the form of resistance to corporate norms.

ELSA: When we think about an induction process, we weren't happy with the one provided by [their governing body] ... We're a very different service. And I think the more services we visit we really know how different we are ... When we think about our own service – what we can do in here, I mean, it's really boundless. We can go for it!

(Elsa, interview 2, lines 119–123)

This increased confidence was likely attributable to Elsa and Rebecca's realization that the *knowledge* available to them among their colleagues was sufficient to address problems of practice. As Elsa said, "Instead of bringing in all these outside people, let's use our people, because there's amazing skills."

7.7.3 *Effective Leadership Builds Workplace Solidarity*

For Elsa and Rebecca, this awareness of the knowledge available to them also resulted in increased *solidarity*. This shift was evident when Rebecca described the recruitment of a new Room Leader for the center that was being carried out at the time of the interview:

REBECCA: We've had a few interviews. But we've just found it's not the right person. Whereas prior to when I first started, I think it was just, "Yeah, fill in the position." Whereas now, we know exactly what we want. And who we want. And that will best suit our team.

(Rebecca, interview 2, lines 242–245)

Elsa had also mentioned, "And now when we think about our core team, we can focus on things like strong pedagogy when people enter our team" (Elsa, interview 2, lines 227–229).

This suggests that, by bringing the nature of their preferred practices to the forefront, the team at Haneul Early Learning Center had developed a stronger sense of their shared cultural norms and expectations, one of which had become to ensure that the "right" people were employed. A related shift was that the number of staff in the center had decreased (from around thirty-five to fewer than twenty-five) without decreasing the number of enrollments. This was achieved by reducing the engagement of casual and part-time staff. One possibility is that, by becoming conscious of the work involved in engaging new staff, the center had (either consciously or unconsciously) moved to a policy of ensuring more stable and full-time staffing.

7.7.4 Effective Leadership Exerts Influence

By the time of the second interview, Haneul Early Learning Center's success in practice development was spreading to other centers under their governing body.

REBECCA: Yeah, and we definitely have had visitors from other centers as well. Center Directors, teachers – that have come for a visit and been with us for a couple of days and so on. And they actually walk away with some of our practices that we've implemented. And documentation as well. So, they've requested that. And that's fine. We share our knowledge and that's what us teachers do. We're also there as a helping hand for our other services and centers around us.

(Rebecca, interview 2, lines 149–153)

Again, it is worth pausing to recognize the achievements of Elsa, Rebecca, and their colleagues who, as recently as eighteen months beforehand, had been asked to address twenty-four aspects of the center's work that were not complying with regulatory requirements. Achievements at Haneul Early Learning Center during the formative intervention had transformed the way the center was viewed by others.

ELSA: And it's not until, as [Rebecca] said, people actually visit and spend time with us. And they'd say, "I thought you guys were crap. Like, I thought you guys were terrible." ... But now, we're in a good space. [Our governing body] is funneling people to us to say, "Go and learn from Haneul. They are doing this really well. And go and observe. Go and learn." Whereas we were [the ones] doing a lot of that [before now].

(Elsa, interview 2, lines 263–268)

7.7.5 Effective Leadership Focuses on Systems of Practice, not Attitudes of Persons

In their first interview, Elsa and Rebecca revealed a strong emphasis on a perceived need to change the knowledge and dispositions of individual colleagues. However, by focusing on systemic (rather than personal) change, their attention had shifted toward the quality of center *practice* at a *systemic* level.

ELSA: I think the biggest thing I learned from [the Change Laboratories was to] remove the people. Think [instead] about the practice and the object of it. Because otherwise you get bogged down in the person thing . . . Personally, that has been beneficial for my ongoing professional development. Just thinking, "Okay, stop. Let's think about the object happening here. Let's not think about the person. And let's move forward with that." And it can create a bit of a different lens.

(Elsa, interview 2, lines 282–287)

There is an apparent irony here that Elsa is talking about what has been "personally" helpful for her in learning to think systemically. Rebecca added that, "I think for me personally it's provided me with a tool to reflect even deeper on my practices. And my role and responsibility" (Rebecca, interview 2, lines 288–289). But these are not paradoxical findings because, as explained in Chapter 6, CHAT scholars understand individual and social development to be simultaneous and co-evolving. Haneul Early Learning Center has developed through input from Elsa and Rebecca, but at the same time they have developed in their individual leadership capacities.

7.7.6 Effective Leadership Respects History but Looks to the Future

Elsa and Rebecca were under no illusions about what they had achieved through their participation in the Change Laboratories and the intervention they had led at Haneul Early Learning Center. These understandings were contextualized by an awareness of the center's "dark history:"

ELSA: We are really thirsty for knowledge and I think sometimes we've felt that [working at] Haneul can be a barrier, because there is so much dark history. So, it was ploughing through all of that baggage to sometimes then get to the new learning . . . And we obviously took this role on knowing that there would be that sort of stuff. But then sometimes it gets heavy. And thinking, "Oh man, are we having to go through the planning cycle again?!" And [we] weren't able to take the next step forward into something new. But now it's like a –

REBECCA: – yeah, I think we can obviously say we can see the light –
ELSA: – oh yeah –
REBECCA: – at the end of the tunnel –
ELSA: – and that totally helps.

(Elsa and Rebecca, interview 2, lines 370–380)

In contrast to their previous sense of the burdensome history of practices in the center, Elsa and Rebecca were now creatively and optimistically engaged in imagining what future practices might look like, a practice Sannino (2022) called "warping" – the practice of casting forward an anchor from a fishing boat and working toward it, or using an anchor to stabilize one's situation in a stormy sea:

> A successfully implemented second stimulus in TADS [transformative agency by double stimulation] may be understood as a warping anchor that hits the ground and allows the vessel to move forward. Actions of throwing the kedge anchor are made in the attempt to find suitable ground. These are search actions. Only when the kedge is hooked to the ground does the crew regain control of the situation allowing them to pull the vessel out of harm's way. These are taking-over actions: the vessel is still in the troubled area, but the crew are able to manoeuvre it. Breaking-out actions occur when the vessel is moved away from the problem area. (Sannino, 2022, p. 12)

It seems fitting, then, to finish this chapter with Elsa's description (interview 2, lines 459–467) of casting forward into the future, despite the inevitability of ongoing turbulence of life in an early childhood education service.

ELSA: It's not us saying, "This is the way, and this is the road, and we know all because we're the Educational Leaders." It's, "Come on this journey with us." ... In terms of forward anchoring, when I think about our role now, I like to think that might be more of what we do. We think about what Haneul might look like in the future. And what is that journey, and what is our role going to be on that journey?

CHAPTER 8

A Conversation between Approaches
No Gifts, No Comparisons, Just Enough Food for Thought
He whakawhiti whakaaro korero

Anne, Joce, and Arvay

In this final chapter, we engage with how we might, with our readers, make sense of this volume as a whole. We began this book, both as the artefact now before you and the process of coauthorship, in a spirit of curiosity, inclusion, and resistance:

- **Curiosity.** What have we learned about each other? What have we learned about our theoretical and methodological choices as researchers? Can this collection of such diverse theories and methods make a sensible contribution to the literature on leadership in early childhood education?
- **Inclusion.** How did we manage to work across our three different home languages? How were our diverse cultural backgrounds brought into conversation with each other? How have the chapters reflected our desire for cultural, linguistic, and scientific inclusion in our descriptions of the work of leaders?
- **Resistance.** What established and nascent discourses of leadership in early childhood education have we brought into question? What has been embraced and what has been resisted within our theoretical and methodological choices? How might we continue to resist the temptation to foreclose on "what works" for leaders and leadership in early childhood education?

These and other questions have formed the material for multiple conversations among the three of us as this book was written – all in the online context imposed by a global pandemic – and we return to these three themes in the second half of this chapter. We begin the chapter by returning to the core claims of the Think Tank Manifesto, outlined in Chapter 1, that provided the starting point for our collaboration, and reflect on some of the ways we have tried to illustrate these convictions through this volume, before returning to the themes of curiosity, inclusion, and resistance.

8.1   Revisiting Our Manifesto

1. That the field of early childhood education is entitled to decolonize, reclaim, and shape the nature of its professionalism and to conceptualize multiple professionalisms. As a reader of this volume, you may have searched in vain for a definitive explanation of what constitutes a "leader" in early childhood education. Instead, we have presented a variety of groups and individuals whose only common characteristic is that they are charged with influencing the practices of their colleagues in the interests of more inclusive educational environments for children and families. Arvay's work, for example, demonstrates the consequences of lack of inclusion for center leaders and underscores the need for early childhood services to be aware of the ongoing effects of colonization of land, thought and actions, particularly for leaders. In all our case studies, the participants begin from the perspective of what *they* know about professionalism and professional practice, not from a unitary definition of what and who counts as a leader.

2. That the field has its own distinctive body of knowledge drawn from multiple and diverse representations of knowledge. Despite the cultural and linguistic differences between Aotearoa New Zealand, Australia, and Norway, early childhood education has its own distinctive artefacts and cultural norms that can be found in all three countries and, indeed, anywhere extrafamilial care of very young children takes place. This is due, in part, to the ongoing normative effects of the edicts handed down by the founders of the early childhood education movement. By contrast, the cases we have presented have their origins, respectively, in the prehistory and cosmology of Māori society, the rhizomatic imagination of Continental philosophy, and the Marxian psychology of twentieth-century Russia, not in the child-centered, play-based typologies of dominant early childhood education practices. Nevertheless, we have shown how each of these theoretical traditions can speak in productive ways to the established cultural forms of early childhood education. Joce's work, for example, demonstrates the way the cultural norms of early childhood education can be brought to conscious awareness and treated as malleable within a professional development process for leaders. Practices that have been historically treated as "true" become, once again, provisional and open to question.

3. That leaders and leadership are not a panacea for any "quality crisis" that has overtaken the early childhood field. A distinctive feature of all three of our cases is that they assume leadership to be a collective social practice, even as leadership "touches down" in individual leaders. This is not simply an artefact of the way we each work methodologically; it is an attempt to resist placing the burden of demands to improve the quality of early childhood education provision principally on the shoulders of leaders. Furthermore, our interests are not with heroic and charismatic (typically male) individual leaders, not least because this type of leadership is not characteristic of the history of the early childhood field. Quality, however defined, has always been determined collectively in early childhood education, even as it is increasingly represented through national policy agendas. For example, the teachers with whom Anne has worked show how early childhood education quality is, at its core, found in daily engagements between children and educators, and they show how leaders can facilitate a collective awareness of these engagements.

4. That leadership in early childhood education must resist the binaries that contribute to polarizations in education and wider society. We have written this book at a time when social, economic, and cultural polarities have been exacerbated by a global existential threat that, paradoxically, has demonstrated how the binaries that underpin late capitalism (east|west, rich|poor, imperial|colonized, safe|at risk, young|old, black|white, left|right, north|south, leaders|followers) threaten to overwhelm our planet. Curiosity, as well as critique, is essential in the ongoing work of overcoming the negative effects of such binaries. Anne's case study documents how early childhood leaders and educators can develop the confidence to think otherwise and to interrogate long-held assumptions about the world with professionalism and respect. Critically, her work critiques potential binaries in early childhood education between "leaders" and "followers."

5. That the work of leadership is a site for making and remaking identity, subjectivity, self-determination, and difference for individual leaders and groups of leaders. Even as the leaders in each of our case studies bend to the task of supporting and developing others, they themselves are experiencing – and trying to make sense of – their own cultural inheritances, social situations, and developing capability. In all three case studies, the participating leaders were grappling with the effects of change, driven to a greater or lesser degree by policy systems outside of their direct influence, and the case studies each reflect the additional social and emotional burden that change can impose on leaders. For the leaders in Arvay's study, their story of change extends from precolonization, even ancient times, through to the present day.

6. That leadership in early childhood education must not only critique continuity but also contest the nature and effects of change. As Joce points out in Chapter 6, an adherence to continuity can result in sedimentation of unhelpful ideas and practices. However, this does not automatically imply that all change is good. Leaders in early childhood education are charged with leading change, whether from within their organizations or as a consequence of external changes in policy, funding, or the needs of local communities. In our case studies, we reflect a range of timescales, from the enduring effects of almost two centuries of colonization for Arvay's research participants, Anne's sustained work with one center across several years, and Joce's case study of a professional development program across just six months. Yet each of these timescales reflects both continuity and change and, in each of three case studies, we adopt methodological techniques to try to capture a sense of change across time. Studies of leadership in early childhood education that confine themselves to single phenomena (identity, professionalism) or single methods (often self-report generated through semistructured interviews) may have reached the limits of their usefulness. To make sense of continuity and change in early childhood education and its leaderships, multiple methods are needed and they should be applied across extended timescales. Reaching beyond the familiar for educational researchers, we wonder about the potential of inter-disciplinary and multidisciplinary research to interrogate continuity and change in leadership even further and more deeply.

7. That leadership confers a particular responsibility to examine more deeply the problems of society that reach into early childhood education including injustice, harmful consumption, and the suppression of diversity in all its forms. Every leader involved in the case studies reported here understands that having been given a leadership role of some kind, they have a responsibility to do something with it. In the first instance, this may be to smooth the way for new staff in the interests of improving the center program (Joce's case study) or opening up work with children for examination and reflection (Anne's case study). Leaders in early childhood education may also feel a wider responsibility to their community and culture that is intrinsic to their leadership, not separate from it (as in Arvay's case study). The outgrowths of these responsibilities may present themselves as pragmatic changes in center practice, as the strengthening of ideological positions, as the development of new knowledge, as an increase in kindness, as greater respect for the natural world, as an expression of joy, or in any number of other ways. Individually or taken as a whole, these outgrowths reflect the work of leaders as they collaborate with others to realize possible and inclusive futures.

8.2 Continuing in a Spirit of Curiosity

We warned at the outset that simply presenting a variety of cases in itself would not be sufficient to illustrate the complexity of leadership for the early childhood field. To truly understand this complexity, cases of leadership practice need to be understood as existing in tension with one another, as potentially contestable within and across cases, and open to exploration, adaptation, and even rejection. This requires us as leaders, educators, and researchers to remain curious about our profession and its practices.

Between – and we add within – the cases in this volume there are articulations and distinctions occurring simultaneously. As a consequence, we want to avoid a view of leadership and knowledge about leadership that is seen as being produced in academic isolation or in advance. Rather, we see leadership as always the result of multiplicities and/or bodies coming together in case-assemblages, and assemblages of cases, driven by a curiosity about other ways of seeing the world. In the present chapter, therefore, we neither encourage nor engage in comparisons between different chapters, approaches, cases, theories, and practices. Rather, we hope we have provided sufficient theoretical backcloth to throw different leadership perspectives into relief. We certainly argue for strong theoretical foundations and thoroughness of theoretical application, a constant thinking *with* theory, as an engine to support and drive curiosity about leadership in early childhood education. We do this without staking a claim for one particular theory. Our own selection of theories is the product of our personal and professional histories, the influence of colleagues and others we have encountered, and a sense of "goodness-of-fit" between the research problems we pursue and the theories that might move our thinking forward.

Therefore, we offer no gifts (concepts, programs, methods, meanings, theories, traditions, inheritances), only more and other ways *through which* to move thinking about leadership forward. The answer to the pursuit of quality is not leadership in itself, but a simultaneous troubling and celebration of diverse approaches to understanding work and learning in early childhood education. We encourage reading across these approaches, leaning into the (perhaps inevitable) discomfort arising from whatever differences the reader detects, and striving to engage in dialogues between them in a spirit of curiosity, solidarity, and connectedness.

Our efforts to stay curious and resist foreclosing on the "most effective" forms of leadership come from an awareness that such gifts can be dangerous. Deconstructing the concept of the "Gift," Jacques Derrida (1992) called into question the giving of gifts as someone giving a nice present to someone else. In the context of this book, this would equate to us offering a leadership theory, program, or fixed policy to the reader and suggesting that it be implemented. Derrida noted that "gift" means poison in German (and, we note, also in Norwegian) and traced its origins in the Greek "Phàrmakon" (drug, medicine), an inchoate "charm," "remedy," or "poison" (Derrida, 1981, pp. 131–132). Derrida recognizes that any phenomenon is dependent on alterity – a contrast with the "other" – that can stimulate a sense of threat and call forth the need to mount a defense. Derrida's account ultimately seeks to acknowledge the insidious extent to which a narcissistic self, and its need for conscious or unconscious gratification, may be at work in the act of giving. Despite our accumulated experience of researching leadership in early child-hood education, we make no such gift. Rather we call for the maintenance of curiosity in ourselves and others.

Yet, in the spirit of continuing to lean into the tension between our theoretical positions, in this chapter we offer an alternative interpretation of a gift. In a Te Ao Māori worldview, a gift is referred to as a taonga or treasure, and therefore a rather different interpretation to that shared in this chapter. Taonga is a tikanga Māori principle derived from both a physical and spiritual origin. Taonga are shared as a form of generosity *without the need for reciprocation*, and are valued contributions that add to the wider collective when underpinned by aroha (love). Hence this volume can also be seen as a taonga that is shared with aroha, an act of generosity which has the ability to enhance and present possibilities for leadership.

As an alternative to the concept of a gift, Derrida advocates thinking through *aporias*. An aporia may be understood as a situation in which someone must decide to act in a determined direction without secure knowledge of what the consequences will be. For Derrida, an aporia is a sort of formal negativity, a nonroad "entailing an indeterminable experi-ence" (Derrida, 1993, p. 16), that is concerned with putting into motion new thinking about what might be possible or, more precisely, risking engagement with the possibility of the impossible. This experience of moving forward without secure foresight is a distinctive characteristic of both leadership and teaching.

Derrida talks of the necessity of going through the trial of no less than three aporias. First there is the aporia of *suspension*. For a leadership decision to be just, there must be both a continuity of traditional prece-dent *and* the discontinuity caused by making a fresh judgment with respect to each particular case, situation, employee, child, or activity. In its "proper moment" such a judgment must be both regulated and without regulation: "It must conserve the law and destroy it or suspend it enough to have to reinvent it in each case, rejustify it, at least reinvent it in the reaffirmation and the new and free confirmation of its principle" (Derrida, 2002, p. 55). We concur with Derrida when we suggest that any leadership and leadership decision cannot be the product of any theoretical machine, but must stem from a fresh reengineering of that machine, demanding both lineage and rupture.

Second, there is the aporia of *undecidability*, hence the aporetic structure of knowledge, or knowledge structured as nonknowledge. This second aporia creates a moment of paralysis of indecision that one has to pass through in order to go on, even without knowing. Here there is the loss of subjective certainty. What one gains, however, is the strength to go on, wanting more. The third aporia is that of *urgency:* we *have* to decide and we *have* to go on. A decision cannot wait, and no decision is also a decision. This situation "is a madness" according to Derrida (1993, p. 63): we have to decide, but a just decision is impossible. However, paradoxically, this mad impossibility is what makes movement beyond paralysis possible; this is both the law and the force of the aporia. In terms of leadership, this is a practice of *living on*; a practice of leadership in a time of promise. The bulwark against despair in the face of constant aporias is curiosity, which understands that practice always occurs on shifting ground as well as understanding the limits of attempts to fix, locate, and define within the bounds of what is already "known."

This aporetic structure leaves the leader to themselves and their will, to act morally together and with others. For something therefore to be given and had, for something to touch and be touched by, it must always pass through aporia. The plural logic of aporia, its formal negativity, impossibility, impossible invention, antinomy, or contradiction from which there is no passage means "its elementary milieu does not allow for something that could be called a passage, step, walk, gate, displacement, or replacement, a kinesis in general" (Derrida, 1993, p. 21). This is a profound challenge for those who research leadership: there can be no gifts given "as such." Rather, there is only a continuous thinking *with* and *in* our theories, leaderships, and actions, conducted in a spirit of generosity and love. Here, because there is no proper name or gift "as such" at all (no word or concept, no leadership theory or school, no narrative, no genre, no story, no text or history to provide an all-encompassing truth), there is nothing to be given or had. There are no oppositions, only possibilities. Therefore, through our book we have shown different leadership models, research approaches, theories, and perspectives purely as food for thought.

8.3 Continuing in a Spirit of Inclusion

The thinking processes we describe are of affective figuring and/or leadership, and of processes of becoming leaders, with the aim of shaping inclusive learning spaces, in terms of both center practices and of research practices. We think this is urgent and fitting for the contemporary interdisciplinary and collaborative leadership education and leadership research culture of a new generation of thinkers and makers. It ultimately represents a reorientation of leadership studies by asking whether the abstractions one attempts, as we try to move from imitation to imagination, are abstract enough in order to think more and other.

After an aporia, we see connections, relations, lines, arrows, circles, and points pop up everywhere. They make fugitive inscriptions on organizations, on theories, policies, leaderships, and practice, which themselves are surfaces that act as canvases for imagery even with ephemeral materials like affects, words, thoughts, dreams, and wishes. Aporia take shape in organizations, in meetings, at home and in in-service education, as well as behind our desks and computers in processes of grasping for knowledge, trying to make sense of what we witness in our educational institutions, our local communities, and close surroundings. We live in a time of radical transformations, experimental solutions, and continuous contestations.

This acceptance of change, incompleteness, and provisionality reorients leadership, and knowledge production in leadership case studies and case study research, to a novel and continuous process of variation and diffusion. It implies a move from a mechanistic approach to leadership toward more open, flexible, and inclusive approaches. Ultimately, our book is a call for exploration and experimentation around a continuum of variation in leadership and knowledge production, thus disrupting processes of reterritorialization by traditionally dominant forms of knowledge. With respect to research, the book thus represents a stepping beyond the endeavor of traditional leadership case studies and case study research to achieve validity. Rather, evaluative categories like care, strength, joy, surprise, interest, and meaning become important. Such categories dissolve the binary division of trustworthy research and nontrustworthy research to recognize the self-organizing properties of data itself and open up all kinds of possibilities for becomings, including possible leadership cases-assemblages, phenomena of interest, cases, and knowledge productions. The intimate and the political are rethought together and mobilized as inclusive practices in research, leadership, and teaching.

A reorientation toward such productive processes and actions is necessary to move leadership studies and case study research on leadership from dealing with the constant to dealing with variation. This calls for a spreading of research interests and case definitions more widely, and hence the production of novel and heterogeneous knowledge without being restricted by the methodological biases of traditional leadership case study research. In particular, such restrictions are seen in critical research designs and a focus on power relations in leadership studies. Unless there are built-in modalities that pay attention to concepts of critique and power, such studies polarize, hierarchize, instrumentalize, reduce and, in the long run, risk destroying leadership studies and research on leadership. Or, put another way, they will cement a deadlock in early childhood leadership and leadership studies. We might see types of individualized, even authoritarian, leaderships emerge that counteract all good intentions of engendering growth in coworkers, or imaginative co-construction of activities and pedagogies, let alone deauthorized processes of democratizing knowledges for inclusion.

The reorientation we suggest in this book makes a call for a creative pluralism of leaderships that simultaneously counteracts any predetermined or controlling "best practice" of leadership. It is a reimagination of leaderships and also a reorientation toward a collective creativity of leaderships. We seek to turn critical studies into studies of critique through making language, caring, and joy all truly actionable. In critique, a problem is just another chance to rethink, think more, think beyond, think over, and engage in deauthorized thinking processes. Barad (2007), building on the work of Jacques Derrida (1930–2004), would call these processes *thinkingfeeling*. Further, through turning power and studies of power into generative work and speculations on force and ethics, researchers can provide generous spaces as a background for exchanges of ideas and experiences, and putting an end to privileging any knowledge, with all bodies involved.

Rather than remark on the contrasts between our approaches, we wonder about the potential of hybrid ontologies to make leaderships and leadership case study research infinitely more complex and unpredictable than more traditional approaches. Such ontologies are inherently political, with the potential to encourage leaders to let go of predefined leadership programs and methodologies and thus open up such programs to processes of deterritorialization in response to questions about what might be good leadership for the early childhood field. We suggest that leaderships, leadership studies, and research be designed along the features of *minor science* (Barad, 2007; Braidotti, 2013; Deleuze & Guattari, 2004 a, b; Reinertsen & Flatås, 2017; Semetsky, 2020; Stengers, 2008; 2018; Thomas & Reinertsen, 2016), offering new possibilities to discover and explore cases – *the betweens* – as well as the flows of affects that produce a desire to lead, or rather leaders who stand in their own mana (prestige).

8.4 Continuing in a Spirit of Resistance

A striking characteristic of all three of the case studies in this book is the way leaders and educators exert agency to resist narratives and discourses that would hinder their range of movement. In Arvay's case study, her participants draw on concepts and enactments of mana, wairua, and tikanga to navigate contexts where the project of colonization continues to be felt. In Anne's case study, the educators overcome their initial shyness in sharing their writing to become articulate recorders of professional successes and difficulties. Transformative agency is central to Joce's methodology, which sees leaders becoming the shapers and creators of their own circumstances, rather than simply responding to those circumstances.

The concept of agency is understood here as people taking action in *difference*, giving rise to constant becomings, as they reconfigure what was and is with what might be. Such actions are understood as a repetitive or iterative affective force. Barad (2007) elaborates:

> *Agency is «doing» or «being» in its intra-activity. It is the enactment of iterative changes to particular practices – iterative reconfigurings of topological manifolds of spacetimematter relations – through the dynamics of intra-activity. Agency is about changing possibilities of change entailed in reconfiguring material-discursive apparatuses of possibilities of bodily production, including the boundary articulations and exclusions that are marked by those practices in the enactment of a causal structure.* (p. 178; italics in original)

Returning to the problems inherent in the Gift, agency too cannot be prescribed or "given" as a particular value, method, or skill; but leaders can learn to notice and experience agency in affective joint activities and other creative contexts. Affective leadership and leadership education hence involve understanding the role of creativity in leadership and leadership education. We suggest it is important for leaders to embrace curiosity, openness, creativity, fantasy, and the ability to foster and imagine possible (other) futures. In this sense, agency is freedom of self-expression in a social community where every participant is accepted for what and who they are. And the participant, in turn, creates an image of the desired future, seeks to learn, explore, make a discovery, understand themself and others. This creativity gives freedom of choice and freedom of action for self-expression. Such freedom is the procedural side of the activity of a leader who wants to advance agency and subjective professionalism.

In a project initiated by the Norwegian government on leadership and quality,[1] the participating leaders were asked the following questions:

1. What do you consider as distractions for you in your efforts to advance quality?
2. What do you consider *not* being a distraction?
3. How do you move behind and beyond distractions?

On the first question the answers were unanimously related to administration. Leaders recounted having been given too many administrative tasks and too much administrative responsibility, but without administrative resources and support. Another distraction they mentioned was the constant flow and distribution of ad hoc tasks, often coming from further up in center systems, with expectations of quick responses and tight timelines. Third on the list was so called worthy causes and good initiatives that were outside of planned activities. These responses arose not from resistance or a reluctance to perform, but from the way their own awareness of these distractions engendered doubts about their own priorities. Fourth, and related, the leaders listed political initiatives from the outside as directly influencing leaders' possibilities for influencing and actually leading their own organizations. What the leaders called for was the possibility of influencing their own organizations and a strengthening of their own positions, being free from forced commitments and activities. What was called for was the opportunity for leaders to focus and not be distracted from what they professionally evaluated as vital and as core factors for success. Their resistance was not to administrative or external requests per se, but to the imposition of priorities from outside that accompanied these requests.

On the question about aspects of their work that were *not* a distraction, the answers revolved around the significance and joy to be found in meetings with other leaders and employees. Such meetings were characterized as open and exploratory or, as was expressed during one observation, "Learning meetings: The right to share thoughts and to follow the

---

[1] Informasjon til barnehageeiere – videreutdanning for barnehagelærere (Information for kindergarten owners – further education for kindergarten teachers), Utdannings-direktoratet (Directorate of Education), www.udir.no.

laughter when it breaks out and when the feet begin to move faster" (Fieldnotes, October 15, 2021). Finally, when asked about how to move behind and beyond distraction, the leaders emphasized the importance of understanding complexity in itself and being given the chance to lead by focusing deeply, instead of just stacking multiple issues, themes, programs, and policies side by side. In other words, "Focus must be piled up, not distributed and just put side by side" (Fieldnotes, October 15, 2021).

The leaders were questioned further about this issue of focus and the concept of attention:

1. What deserves your attention as leader in your organization?
2. How can you stretch your attention as leader toward quality?

The discussion quickly turned to the importance of "catching one another in the act of doing something good" (Fieldnotes, October 15, 2021), because this "catching" has the effect of multiplying subsequent good outcomes. Further, and significantly, the leaders stressed the importance of taking thoughts and images of perfection and "the perfect" out of their vocabularies. They understood that, by resisting perfection, they made it less dangerous for themselves and their colleagues to learn and do something new. This might appear as something of a risk for leaders: Will they be subject to erasure if they turn their colleagues' attention outward and away from themselves as the leader and on to the world? The answer here is in the need to not only resist perfection, but to resist the temptation to always know what is *right*. Rather, thinking about what is *good* allows us to think about moral virtues as something whose reality is manifest in everyday leadership and research encounters, in concrete cases of moral virtue – for instance, in acts of vulnerability, honesty, and kindness. Certainly, such thinking can lead to high-flying speculation, but it always demands a return to our sensual worlds and everyday worries. This resistance to the need to feel one is "getting it right" is a hugely challenging task but arguably exactly what is needed today to extend complex figurations of early childhood education and care in contemporary leadership studies and research.

Here we finally and ultimately speak of resisting the self. Novelist and philosopher Iris Murdoch (1919–1999) borrowed the term "attention" from philosopher Simone Weil (1909–1943), and hence the idea of being attentive as holding a just and loving gaze directed upon an individual reality. This "just vision" requires what Murdoch called "unselfing," a sort of dismantling of oneself in a quantum space in order to realize that something other than oneself is real. This calls for a resistance to accepted subject positions as leaders, looking instead for new forms of inclusive leaderships, efforts to constantly reauthor knowledges and rights, and an understanding of knowledges and rights as political struggles integral to knowledge creation, knowing, and learning. In this book we have tried to acknowledge the existence of different ontologies while also acknowledging that they each can demonstrate leadership as constant continuation of both acceptance and resistance.

8.5   Concluding Thoughts

Our presentation of three case studies from the perspective of three markedly different theoretical frameworks is part of our plea for research and practice in leadership in early childhood education to resist reductive narratives of right and wrong, compliance and control. In times of national curriculum frameworks and quality assessment standards, we seek to create openings toward expanded meaning fields that nourish valuable diversities of ontoepistemic cultures. There are much larger imaginary and creative sources to draw from than those presented here. We acknowledge that, even as engagement with theory increases levels of intimacy in understanding specific cases, it can also lead to possible feelings of unease. Perhaps that has been your experience in reading this volume, yet we venture to hope that you have also experienced possibilities within and between these different ways of knowing.

Through our manifesto, the questions we posed for readers in Chapter 1, and our articulations of theory and empirical cases, we seek to advocate for a rich and complex view of leadership and leadership training and research. In particular, we encourage movement away from centered views of learning focused on identity and individuality, toward decentered views that look to collective ontologies and subjective becomings. We think our research shows that this type of leadership, and research into leadership, can support creative pluralism in organizations, education, and research, while simultaneously counteracting predetermined and controlling views of organizational cultures. We trust our engagement in multiplicity can become a strong force for knowledge co-creation toward truly inclusive forms of early childhood education leadership.

References

Andersson, Å., Korp, P., & Reinertsen, A. (2020). Thinking with new materialism in qualitative case studies. *International Journal of Qualitative Methods. 19*, 1–9. https://doi.org/10.1177/1609406920976437

Armstrong-Read, A. (2022). *Te Reo Karanga o Matangireia, The Sacred call of leadership. Wahine Maori perspectives of leadership in early childhood education: The denial of the sacred Karanga of leadership by the persistence of colonisation in mainstream early childhood services in Aotearoa New Zealand* (Unpublished PhD thesis). Monash University.

Attanasio, O. P. (2015). The determinants of human capital formation during the early years of life: Theory measurement and policies. *Journal of the European Economic Association, 13*(6), 949–997. https://doi.org/10.1111/jeea.12159

Australian Children's Education and Care Quality Authority [ACECQA]. (2016). *Educational program and practice. An analysis of Quality Area 1 of the National Quality Standard*. Author.

Avis, J. (2007). Engeström's version of activity theory: A conservative praxis? *Journal of Education and Work, 20*(3), 161–177. https://doi.org/10.1080/13639080701464459

Bakhurst, D. (2009). Reflections on activity theory. *Educational Review, 61*(2), 197–210. https://doi.org/10.1080/00131910902846916

Barad, K. (2007). *Meeting the universe halfway: Quantum physics and the entanglement of matter and meaning*. Duke University Press.

Barlow, C. (1991). *Tikanga whakaaro: Key concepts in Māori cutlure*. Oxford University Press.

Beach, K. (1999). Consequential transitions: A sociocultural expedition beyond transfer in education. *Review of Research in Education, 24*(1), 101–139. https://doi.org/10.3102/0091732X024001101

Becker, H. S. (2014). *What about Mozart? What about murder? Reasoning from cases*. University of Chicago Press.

Best Start (2016, June). *Early childhood development and the childcare crisis* (Briefing Note). Theirworld Children's Charity. https://theirworld.org/resources/briefing-early-childhood-development-and-the-childcare-crisis

Biesta, G. (2020). Risking ourselves in education: Qualification, socialization, subjectification revisited. *Educational Theory, 70*(1), 89–104. https://doi.org/10.1111/edth.12411

Bishop, R. (1995). *Collaborative research stories: Whakawhanaungatanga* (PhD thesis). University of Otago. http://hdl.handle.net/10523/531

(1999). *Kaupapa Maori research: An indigenous approach to creating knowledge.* In N. Robertson (Ed.), *Maori and psychology: Research and practice* (pp. 1–6). Maori and Psychology Research Unit, University of Waikato. https://hdl .handle.net/10289/874

(2003). Changing power relations in education: Kaupapa Maori messages for "mainstream" education in Aotearoa/New Zealand. *Comparative Education, 39*(2), 221–238. https://doi.org/10.1080/03050060302555

(2005). A Māori approach to research and creating knowledge. In N. K. Denzin & Y. S. Lincoln (Eds.), *Handbook of qualitative research* (3rd ed.), pp. 109–135. Sage.

Bishop, R., & Glynn, T. (1999). *Culture counts: Changing power relations in education.* Dunmore Press.

Boyle, T., Grieshaber, S., & Petriwskyj, A. (2018). An integrative review of transitions to school literature. *Educational Research Review, 24,* 170–180. https://doi.org/10.1016/j.edurev.2018.05.001

Braidotti, R. (2010). Elemental complexity and relationality: The relevance of nomadic thought for contemporary science. In P. Gaffner (Ed.), *The force of the virtual: Deleuze, science, and philosophy* (pp. 211–228). University of Minnesota Press.

(2013). *The posthuman.* Polity Press.

(2018). A theoretical framework for the critical posthumanities. *Theory, Culture & Society, 36*(6), 31–61. https://doi.org/10.1177/0263276418771486

Bussey, K., & Hill, D. (2017). Care as curriculum: Investigating teachers' views on the learning in care. *Early child development and care, 187*(1), 128–137. https://doi.org/10.1080/03004430.2016.1152963

Campbell-Barr, V. (2018). The silencing of the knowledge-base in early childhood education and care professionalism. *International Journal of Early Years Education, 26*(1), 75–89. https://doi:10.1080/09669760.2017.1414689

Cannella, G. S., & Viruru, R. (2003). (Euro-American constructions of) education of children (and adults) around the world: A postcolonial critique. In G. S. Cannella & J. L. Kincheloe (Eds.), *Kidworld: Childhood studies, global perspectives, and education* (pp. 197–214). Peter Lang.

Carlson, D. L., McGuire, K., Koro-Ljungberg, M., & Cannella, G. (2020). Twisted liminalities *Qualitative Inquiry, 26*(8–9), 1056–1059. https://doi .org/10.1177/1077800420939865

Cheeseman, S., & Walker, R. (Eds). (2019). *Pedagogies for leading practice.* Routledge.

Christie, N. (2009). *Små ord for store spørsmål* [*Small words for big questions*]. Universitetsforlaget.

Clark, R. M. (2012). "I've never thought of myself as a leader but...": The early years professional and catalytic leadership. *European Early Childhood Education Research Journal, 20*(3), 391–401. https://doi.org/10.1080/ 1350293X.2012.704762

Coleman, A., Sharp, C., & Handscomb, G. (2016). Leading highly performing children's centres: Supporting the development of the "accidental leaders." *Educational Management Administration & Leadership, 44*(5), 775–793. https://doi.org/10.1177/1741143215574506

Cram, F. (1993). *Ethics in Māori research.* In L. W. Nikora (Ed.), *Cultural justice and ethics* (pp. 28–30). Psychology Department, University of Waikato. https://hdl.handle.net/10289/3316

Daniels, H. (2001). *Vygotsky and pedagogy.* Routledge Falmer.

Davis, K., Krieg, S., & Smith, K. (2014). Leading otherwise: Using a feminist-poststructuralist and postcolonial lens to create alternative spaces for early childhood educational leaders. *International Journal of Leadership in Education, 18*(2), 1–18. https://doi:10.1080/13603124.2014.943296

Deleuze, G. (1988). *Spinoza: Practical philosophy* (R. Hurley, Trans.). City Lights Books.

(1989). *Cinema 2: The time-image* (H. Tomlinson & R. Galeta, Trans.). University of Minnesota Press.

(1993). *The fold: Leibniz and the Baroque* (T. Conley, Trans.). University of Minnesota Press.

(1994). *Difference and repetition.* Columbia University Press.

(1998). *Essays, clinical and critical.* Verso New Left Books.

(2002a). The actual and the virtual (E. R. Albert, Trans.). In G. Deleuze & C. Parnet (Eds.), (H. Tomlinson, B. Habberjam, & E. R. Albert, Trans), *Dialogues II* (pp. 148–152). Columbia University Press.

(2002b). Dead psychoanalysis: Analyse. In G. Deleuze, & C. Parnet, C (Eds.), (H. Tomlinson, B. Habberjam, & E. R. Albert, Trans.), *Dialogues II* (pp. 77– 119). Columbia University Press.

(2002c). On the superiority of Anglo-American literature. In G. Deleuze & C. Parnet (Eds.), (H. Tomlinson, B. Habberjam, & E. R. Albert, Trans.), *Dialogues II* (pp. 36– 76). Columbia University Press.

(2005). *Pure immanence. Essays on a life.* Zone Books.

Deleuze, G., & Guattari, F. (1994). *What Is philosophy?* (H. Tomlinson & G. Burchell, Trans.). Columbia University Press.

(2004a). *Anti-Oedipus: Capitalism and schizophrenia.* Continuum.

(2004b). *A thousand plateaus: Capitalism and schizophrenia.* Continuum.

Derrida, J. (1981). *Dissemination.* Continuum.

(1992). *Given time.* University of Chicago Press.

(1993). *Aporias.* Stanford University Press.

(2002). *Lovens makt.* Spartakus.

Douglass, A. (2019). *Leadership for quality early childhood education and care.* (Working Paper No. 211). OECD.

Douglas-Huriwai, C. (2012). Māori spirituality: A wairua on auto-pilot? http://craccum.ausa.auckland.ac.nz/?p=1578

Durie, M. (1994). *Whaiora: Māori health development.* Oxford University Press.

(1995). Te Hoe Nuku Roa framework: A Māori identity measure. *Journal of the Polynesian Society, 104*(4), 461–470.

Ellis, V. (2011). Reenergising professional creativity from a CHAT perspective: Seeing knowledge and history in practice. *Mind, Culture, and Activity, 18*(2), 181–193. https://doi.org/10.1080/10749039.2010.493595

Engeström, Y. (1987). *Learning by expanding: An activity-theoretical approach to developmental research.* Orienta-Konsultit.

(1993). Developmental studies of work as a testbench of activity theory: The case of primary care medical practice. In S. Chaiklin & J. Lave (Eds.), *Understanding practice: Perspectives on activity and context* (pp. 64–103). Cambridge University Press.

(1999). Innovative learning in work teams: Analysing cycles of knowledge creation in practice. In Y. Engeström, R. Miettinen, & R. Punamaki (Eds.), *Perspectives on activity theory* (pp. 377–404). Cambridge University Press.

Engeström, Y., & Sannino, A. (2010). Studies of expansive learning: Foundations, findings and future challenges. *Educational Research Review, 5*, 1–24. https://doi.org/10.1016/j.edurev.2009.12.002

Escayg, K.-A. (2020). Anti-racism in U.S. early childhood education: Foundational principles. *Sociology Compass, 14*(4), e12764. https://doi.org/10.1111/soc4.12764

Fasoli, L., Scrivens, C., & Woodrow, C. (2007). Challenges for leadership in Aotearoa / New Zealand and Australian early childhood contexts. In L. Keesing-Styles & H. Hedges (Eds.), *Theorising early childhood practice: Emerging dialogues* (pp. 231–253). Pademelon Press.

Ferreira Lemos, M., & Engeström, Y. (2018). Collective concept formation in educational management: An intervention study in São Paulo, Brazil. *Eesti Haridusteaduste Ajakiri, 6*(1), 32–56. https://doi.org/10.12697/eha.2018.6.1.02a

Fitzgerald, T. (2003). Changing the deafening silence of indigenous women's voices in educational leadership. *Journal of Educational Administration, 41*(1), 9–23. https://doi.org/10.1108/09578230310457402

(2006). Walking between two worlds: Indigenous women and educational leadership. *Educational Management Administration and Leadership, 34*(2), 201–213. https://doi.org/10.1177/1741143206062494

(2010). Spaces in-between: Indigenous women leaders speak back to dominant discourses and practices in educational leadership. *International Journal of Leadership in Education, 13*(1), 93–105. https://doi.org/10.1080/13603120903242923

Frankenberg, R. (1993). *Displacing whiteness: Essays in social and cultural criticism.* Duke University Press.

Freedman, S., & Freedman, J. M. (2020). *Becoming a library leader: Seven stages of leadership development for academic librarians.* Association of College and Research Libraries.

Gillham, B. (2000). *The research interview.* Continuum.

Giroux, H. (1998). Youth, memory work, and the racial politics of whiteness. In J. Kincheloe, S. Steinberg, N. Rodriguez, & R. Chennault (Eds.), *White reign: Deploying whiteness in America* (pp. 121–136). St Martin's Griffin.

Gordon-Burns, D., & Campbell, L. (2014). Indigenous rights in Aotearoa/New Zealand–Inakitia rawatia hei kakano mō āpōpō: Students' encounters with bicultural commitment. *Childhood Education, 90*(1), 20–28. https://doi.org/10.1080/00094056.2014.872506

Grosz, E. (2017). *The incorporeal: Ontology, ethics, and the limits of materialism.* Columbia University Press.

Guattari, F. (2008). *The three ecologies.* Continuum.

Halpern, C., Szecsi, T., & Mak, V. (2021). "Everyone can be a leader": Early childhood education leadership in a center serving culturally and linguistically diverse children and families. *Early Childhood Education Journal, 49*(4), 669–679. doi:10.1007/s10643-020-01107-8

Hard, L. (2006). Horizontal violence in early childhood education and care: Implications for leadership enactment. *Australasian Journal of Early Childhood Education, 31*(3), 40–48. https://doi.org/10.1177/183693910603100307

Harvey, D. (2014). *Seventeen contradictions and the end of capitalism.* Profile Books.

Heffernan, M., & Preiss, B. (2020, March 25). "Torn all day, every day": Childcare workers' dilemma amid coronavirus. *The Age.* www.theage.com.au/national/victoria/torn-all-day-every-day-childcare-workers-dilemma-am id-coronavirus-20200325-p54dtl.html

Heikka, J., & Waniganayeke, M. (2011). Pedagogical leadership from a distributed perspective within the context of early childhood education. *International Journal of Leadership in Education: Theory and Practice, 14*(4), 499–512. https://doi.org/10.1080/13603124.2011.577909

Heikka, J., Waniganayake, M., & Hujala, E. (2013). Contextualizing distributed leadership within early childhood education: Current understandings, research evidence and future challenges. *Educational Management, Administration and Leadership, 40*(1), 30–44. https://doi.org/10.1177/1741143212462700

Hohepa, M. (2013). Educational leadership and indigeneity: Doing things the same, differently. *American Journal of Education, 119*(4), 617–631. www.jstor.org/stable/10.1086/670964

Hond-Flavell, E., Ratima, M., Tamati, A., Korewha, H., & Edwards, W. (2017). *Te Kura Mai i Tawhiti: He Tau Kawekawea – Building the foundation for Whanau educational success and wellbeing: A kaupapa Maori ECE approach.* www.tlri.org.nz/sites/default/files/projects/TLRI%20Summary_Hond-Flavell%20web%20ready.pdf

Irwin, K. (1994). Maori research methods and practices. *Sites, 28*(Autumn), 25–43.

Jones, C., Hadley, F., Waniganayake, M., & Johnstone, M. (2019). Find your tribe! Early childhood educators defining and identifying key factors that support their workplace wellbeing. *Australasian Journal of Early Childhood,* *44*(4), 326–338. https://doi.org/10.1177/1836939119870906

Katene, S. (2013). *The spirit of Māori leadership.* Huia.

Krieg, S., Davis, K., & Smith K. A. (2014). Exploring the dance of early childhood educational leadership. *Australasian Journal of Early Childhood,* *39*(1), 73–80. https://doi.org/10.1177/183693911403900110

Lee, J. (2009). Decolonising Māori narratives: Pūrākau as a method. *MAI Review,* *2*(Article 3).

Leont'ev, A. N. (1978). *Activity, consciousness, and personality* (M. J. Hall, Trans.). Prentice-Hall.

Levant, A. (2018). Two, three, many strands of activity theory! *Educational Review, 70*(1), 100–108. https://doi.org/10.1080/00131911.2018.1388619

Longley, J. M. (2020). Embracing LGBTQIA+ staff in early childhood programs. *YC Young Children, 75*(2), 66–73.

Lu, H., & Baker, C. (2014). White knights: Leadership as the heroicisation of whiteness. *Leadership, 12*(4), 420–448. https://doi.org/10.1177/174271501 4565127

Mahon, R. (2010). After neo-liberalism?: The OECD, the World Bank and the child. *Global Social Policy, 10*(2), 172–192. https://doi.org/10.1177/ 1468018110366615

Mahuika, R. (2008). Kaupapa Māori is critical and anti-colonial. *MAI Review, 3*(4), 1–16.

Mahuika, N. (2012). "Kōrero Tuku Iho": reconfiguring oral history and oral tradition (PhD thesis). University of Waikato. https://hdl.handle.net/10289/ 6293

Malone, B. G., & Caddell, T. A. (2000). A crisis in leadership: Where are tomorrow's principals? *The Clearing House: A Journal of Educational Strategies, Issues and Ideas, 73*(3), 162–144. https://doi.org/10.1080/00098650009600938

Manning, E. (2019, September 16). *The minor gesture in 16 movements.* Lecture, Østfold University College.

Marsden, M. (2003). *The woven universe. Selected writings of Rev. Māori Marsden.* The estate of Rev. Māori Marsden.

Marx, K. (1845). Theses on Feuerbach: Thesis 11. In *Marx /Engels selected works* (Vol. 1). [Original pamphlet publication, 1888].

Massumi, B. (1987). Notes on the translation and acknowledgments. In G. Deleuze, G & F. Guattari, *A thousand plateaus: Capitalism and schizophrenia* (pp. xvi–xix). University of Minnesota Press.

(2002). *Parables for the virtual: Movement, affect, sensations.* Duke University Press.

(2010). On critique. *Inflexions 4 – Transversal Fields of Experience* (November 2010), 337–340. www.inflexions.org

(2015). *Politics of affect.* Polity Press.

McIntosh, P. (1989). White privilege: Unpacking the invisible knapsack. *Peace and Freedom, 49*(2), 31–36. https://nationalseedproject.org/Key-SEED-Texts/white-privilege-unpacking-the-invisible-knapsack

Mead, H. (2016). *Tikanga Maori: Living by Māori values.* Huia.

Meadows, M. (2002). *White teachers, white children, white schools: Multiculturalism in geographically homogeneous communities.* Indiana State University.

Melamed, C. (2016). *Women's work: Mothers, children and the global childcare crisis: Policy brief.* Overseas Development Institute.

Miettinen, R. (2013). Creative encounters and collaborative agency in science, technology and innovation. In K. Thomas & J. Chan (Eds.), *Handbook of research on creativity* (pp. 435–444). Edward Elgar.

Miettinen, R., Paavola, S., & Pohjola, P. (2012). From habituality to change: Contribution of activity theory and pragmatism to practice theories. *Journal for the Theory of Social Behaviour, 42*(3), 345–360. https://doi.org/10.1111/j.1468-5914.2012.00495.x

Mikaere, A. (1994). Māori women: Caught in the contradictions of a colonised reality. *Waikato Law Review, 6,* 126–149. www.nzlii.org/nz/journals/WkoLawRw/1994/6.html

Ministry of Education. (2017). *Te Whariki. He whariki matauranga mo nga mokopuna o Aotearoa: Early childhood curriculum.* Ministry of Education.

Molander, A., & Terum, L. I. (2008). *Profesjonsstudier [Profession studies].* Universitetsforlaget.

Morselli, D., & Sannino, A. (2021). Testing the model if double stimulation in a Change Laboratory. *Teaching and Teacher Education, 97.* https://doi.org/10.1016/j.tate.2020.103224

Murphy, N. (2017). *Te Awa Atua. Menstruation in the pre-colonial Māori world.* Whakatane He Puna Manawa.

Nepe, T. (1991). E hao ne e tenei reanga: Te toi huarewa tipuna, Kaupapa Māori, an educational intervention (Master's thesis). University of Auckland. https://researchspace.auckland.ac.nz/docs/uoa-docs/rights.htm

Nicholson, J. (2017). *Emphasizing social justice and equity in leadership for early childhood: Taking a postmodern turn to make complexity visible.* Lexington Press.

Norwegian Ministry of Education and Research. (2018–2019). *Long-term plan for research and higher education 2019–2028.* Author. www.regjeringen.no/no/dokumenter/meld.-st.-4-20182019/id2614131

Nuttall, J. (2022). Formative interventions and the ethics of double stimulation for transformative agency in professional practice. *Pedagogy, Culture and Society, 30*(1), 111–128. https://doi.org/10.1080/14681366.2020.1805498

Nuttall, J., Henderson, L., Wood, E. A., & Trippestad, T. A. (2020). Policy rhetorics and responsibilization in the formation of early childhood educational leaders in Australia. *Journal of Education Policy.* https://doi:10.1080/02680939.2020.1739340

Omdal, H., & Roland, P. (2020). Possibilities and challenges in sustained capacity-building in early childhood education and care (ECEC) institutions: ECEC leaders' perspectives. *European Early Childhood Education Research Journal, 28*(4), 568–581. http://dx.doi.org/10.1080/1350293X.2020.1783929

Ord, K., Mane, J., Smorti, S., Carroll-Lind, J., Robinson, L., Armstrong-Read, A., ... Jalal, J. (2013). *Te whakapakari kaiārahi āhuatanga ako kōhungahunga: Developing pedagogical leadership in early childhood education.* Te Tari Puna Ora o Aotearoa/NZ Childcare Association.

Patterson, A. (2014). *Leadership evolution: From technical expertise to strategic leadership.* Business Expert Press.

Pere, R. (1991). *Te Wheke a celebration of infinite wisdom.* Ao Ako Global Learning New Zealand.

Pihama, L. (1994). Are films dangerous? A Maori women's perspective on *The Piano. Hecate, 20*(2), 239–242.

(2001). Tihei mauriora, honouring our voices, mana wahine as a Kaupapa Māori theoretical framework (PhD thesis). University of Auckland. https://researchspace.auckland.ac.nz/docs/uoa-docs/rights.htm

(2010). Kaupapa Māori theory: Transforming theory in Aotearoa. *He Pukenga Korero, 9*(2), 5–14.

Pihama, L., Cram, F., & Walker, S. (2002). Creating methodological space: A literature review of Kaupapa Māori research. *Canadian Journal of Native Education, 26,* 30–43.

Rains, F. (1998). Is the benign really harmless? Deconstructing some "benign" manifestations of operationalized White privilege. In J. Kincheloe, S. Steinberg, N. Rodriguez, & R. Chennault (Eds.), *White reign: Deploying whiteness in America* (pp. 77–102). St Martin's Griffin.

Rameka, L. (2012). Te whatu kakahu: Assessment in Kaupapa Māori early childhood practice (PhD thesis). University of Waikato, Research Commons. https://hdl.handle.net/10289/6597

Reinertsen, A. B. (2014). Becoming with data: Developing self-assessing recursive pedagogies in schools and using second-order cybernetics as thinking tool. *Policy Futures in Education, 12*(2), 310–322. https://doi.10.2304/pfie.2014.12.2.310

(2018). Unconscious activisms and the subject as critic: A slam articlepoem. In A. Cutter-Mackenzie, K. Malone, & E. Barratt Hacking (Eds.), *Research handbook on childhoodnature* (pp. 295–309). Springer International Handbooks of Education. https://doi.org/10.1007/978-3-319-51949-4_22-1

(2019). The end of criticism producing unconscious: Non-personal activist academic writing. In L. M. Thomas & A. B. Reinertsen (Eds.), *Academic writing and identity constructions: Performativity, space and territory in academic workplaces* (pp. 31–54). SpringerNature, Palgrave Macmillan.

(2020). Fuzzytechie languaging and consilience: Dataphilosophy and transdisciplinary digital force for justice. *Policy Futures in Education, 18*(4), 453–466. https://doi.org/10.1177/1478210319900599

(2021). The art of not knowing; The position of non-knowledge as activisms. *International Review of Qualitative Research, 14*(3), 476–482. https://doi.org/10.1177/1940844720948067

(2022). Storying other than the neoliberal criticism: Cause I have a hunch of something being wrong here. In C. Blyth & T. K. Aslanian (Eds.), *Storying in early childhood education research and practice – posthuman and autoethnographic approaches* (pp. 91–108). Springer Nature.

Reinertsen, A. B., & Flatås, B. (2017). *Ledelse og poesi i barnehagen; Affektive perspektiver i pedagogiske praksiser [Leadership and poetry in Kindergarten; Affective perspectives in pedagogical practises]*. Fagbokforlaget.

Ritchie, J. (2008). Honouring Māori subjectivities within early childhood education in Aotearoa. *Contemporary Issues in Early Childhood, 9*(3), 202–210. https://doi.org/10.2304/ciec.2008.9.3.202

(2014). Contextual explorations of Māori within "Whitestream" early childhood education in Aotearoa New Zealand. In J. Ritchie & M. Skerrett, *Early childhood education in Aotearoa New Zealand: History, pedagogy, and liberation* (pp. 73–91). Palgrave Pivat.

Rodd, J. (2013). *Leadership in early childhood: The pathway to professionalism* (4th ed.). Routledge.

Roitman, J. (2013). *Anti-crisis*. Duke University Press.

Samuelsson, I. P., Wagner, J. T., & Ødegaard, E. E. (2020). The coronavirus pandemic and lessons learning in preschools in Norway, Sweden and the United States: OMEP policy forum. *International Journal of Early Childhood, 52*, 129–144. https://doi.org/10.1007/s13158-020-00267-3

Sannino, A. (2015). The principle of double stimulation: A path to volitional action. *Learning, Culture and Social Interaction, 6*, 1–15. https://doi.org/10.1016/j.lcsi.2015.01.001

(2022). Transformative agency as warping: How collectives accomplish change amidst uncertainty. *Pedagogy, Culture & Society, 30*(1), 9–33. https://doi.org/10.1080/14681366.2020.1805493

Sannino, A., & Engeström, Y. (2017). Co-generation of societally impactful knowledge in Change Laboratories. *Management Learning, 48*(1), 80–96. https://doi.org/10.1177/1350507616671285

Semetsky, I. (2013). Deleuze, edusemiotics, and the logic of affects. In I. Semetsky & D. Masny (Eds.), *Deleuze and Education* (pp. 215–234). Edinburgh University Press.

(2020). Exploring the future form of pedagogy. Education and Eros. In P. P. Trifonas (Ed.), *Handbook of theory and research in cultural studies and education* (pp. 1–11). Springer Nature. https://doi.org/10.1007/978-3-030-01426-1_7-1

Shamir, R. (2008). The age of responsibilization: On market embedded morality. *Economy and Society 37*(1), 1–19. https://doi:10.1080/03085140701760833

Shields, J. C. (1989). Review of *To tell a free story: The first century of Afro-American autobiography, 1760–1865* by William L. Andrews. *Black American Literature Forum, 23*(1), 159–167. https://doi.org/10.2307/2903999

Simondon, G. (1958/2012/2017). *On the mode of existence of technical objects*. Univocal.

Sims, M., Forrest, R., Semann, A., & Slattery, C. (2015). Conceptions of early childhood leadership: Driving new professionalism? *International Journal of*

Leadership in Education, 18(2), 149–166. https://doi.org/10.1080/13603124
.2014.962101

Smeby, J.-C. (2014). Førskolelæreryrket vil neppe utvikle seg til en profesjon [Early childhood work will hardly develop into a profession]. *Første steg, 1*, 12–19.

Smith, G. H. (2003). Kaupapa Maori theory: Theorising indigenous transformation of education and schooling. Paper presentation, Symposium on Kaupapa Maori. Auckland.

(2004). Mai i te Maramatanga, ki te Putanga Mai o te Tahuritanga: From Conscientization to Transformation. *Educational Perspectives, 37*(1), 46–52.

Smith, L. T. (1992). Maori women: Discourse, projects and mana wahine. In S. Middleton & A. Jones (Eds.), *Women and education in Aotearoa: 2* (pp. 33–51). Bridget Williams Books.

(1993). Getting out from down under: Māori women, education and the struggles for mana wāhine. In M. Arnot & K. Weiler (Ed.), *Feminism and social justice in education* (pp. 58–78). Falmer Press.

(1999). *Decolonising methodologies: Research and indigenous peoples.* Zed Books.

(2006). Researching the margins: Issues for Māori researchers. A discussion paper. *Alternative: International Journal of Indigenous Scholarship, 2*(1), 5–27. https://doi.org/10.1177/117718010600200101

(2012). *Decolonizing methodologies, research and indigenous peoples* (2nd ed.). University of Otago Press. Zed Books.

(2021). *Decolonizing methodologies: research and indigenous peoples* (3rd ed.). Zed Books.

Stanley, F. (2020, August 13). Quality childcare can help rebuild our economy. *The Australian.* www.theaustralian.com.au/commentary/quality-childcare-can-help-rebuild-our-economy/news-story/713144625c8ba63de82993efd26 od5ff

Stengers, I. (2008). Experimenting with refrains: Subjectivity and the challenge of escaping modern dualism. *Subjectivity, 22*(1), 38–59. https://doi.org/10 .1057/SUB.2008.6

(2018). *Another science is possible: A manifesto for slow science.* Polity Press.

Stetsenko, A. (2003). Alexander Luria and the cultural-historical activity theory: Pieces for the history of an outstanding collaborative project in psychology. [Review of the book *Alexander Romanovich Luria, a scientific biography*, by E. D. Homskaya]. *Mind, Culture, and Activity, 10*(1), 93–97. https://doi .org/10.1207/S15327884MCA1001_10

Tamati, A., Hond-Flavell, E., & Korewha, H. (2008). *Centre of innovation research report of Te Kopae Piripono.* www.educationcounts.govt.nz/publica tions/ECE/22551/34830

Te Awekotuku, N. (1991). *Mana wahine Maori.* New Women's Press.

Te Kopae Piripono. (2006). Ngā Takohanga e wha. The four responsibilities. www.lead.ece.govt.nz/centersofinnovation

Terrell, A. M., & Allvin, R. E. (2021). Leadership, equity, and NAEYC: There are seats at the table. [El liderazgo, la equidad y NAEYC. Hay lugares en la mesa]. *YC Young Children, 76*(2), 55–58. www.naeyc.org/resources/pubs/yc/summer2021/el-liderazgo-la-equidad

Thomas, L., & Reinertsen, A. B. (2016). Writing matters in leadership practice. *Reconceptualizing Educational Research Methodology 7*(2), 85–100. https://doi.org/10.7577/rerm.1844

Thornton, K. (2019). Leadership in the early years: Challenges and opportunities. *New Zealand Annual Review of Education, 24*, 42–57. https://doi.org/10.26686.nzaroe.v24i0/6327

Tolich, M. (2001). *Research ethics in Aotearoa New Zealand.* Pearson Education.

Tomer, J. F. (2016). *Integrating human capital with human development: The path to a more productive and humane economy.* Palgrave Macmillan.

Vänninen, I., Querol, M. P., & Engeström, Y. (2021). Double stimulation for collaborative transformation of agricultural systems: The role of models for building agency. *Learning, Culture and Social Interaction, 30*, Part A. https://doi.org/10.1016/j.lcsi.2021.100541

Virkkunen, J., & Newnham, D. S. (2013). *The change laboratory: A tool for collaborative development of work and education.* Sense.

Virkkunen, J., & Ristimäki, P. (2012). Double stimulation in strategic concept formation: An activity-theoretical analysis of business planning in a small technology firm. *Mind, Culture, and Activity, 19*(3), 273–286. https://doi.org/10.1080/10749039.2012.688234

Vygotsky, L. S. (1978). *Mind in society: The development of higher psychological processes.* (M. Cole, V. John-Steiner, S. Scribner, & E. Souberman, Eds.). Harvard University Press.

Walker, S. (1996). *Kia tau te rangimarie: Kaupapa Māori theory as a resistance against the construction of Māori as the other* (Unpublished master's thesis). University of Auckland.

Walker, S., Eketone, A., & Gibbs, A. (2006). An exploration of kaupapa Māori research, its principles, processes and applications. *International Journal of Social Research Methodology, 9*(4), 331–344. https://doi.org/10.1080/13645570600916049

Wallace, E. (2018). *Manawanui: Illuminating contemporary meanings of culturally effective social work supervison practice in Te Tai Tokerau, Northland* (Unpublished master's thesis). UNITEC Institute of Technology].

Waniganayake, M. (2014). Being and becoming early childhood leaders: Reflections on leadership studies in early childhood education and the future leadership research agenda. *Journal of Early Childhood Education Research, 3*(1), 65–81.

Waniganayake, M., Cheeseman, S., Fenech, M., Hadley, F., & Shepherd, W. (2012). *Leadership: Contexts and complexities in early childhood education.* Oxford University Press.

Warmington, P. (2008). From "activity" to "labour": Commodification, labour power and contradiction in Engeström's activity theory. *Outlines. Critical Practice Studies, 2*, 4–19. https//doi.org/10.7146/ocps.v10i2.1972

Wertsch, J. V. (2007). Mediation. In H. Daniels, M. Cole, & J. V. Wertsch (Eds.), *The Cambridge companion to Vygotsky* (pp. 178–192). Cambridge University Press.

Whalley, M. E. (2011). Leading and managing in the early years. In L. Miller & C. Cable (Eds.), *Professionalization, leadership and management in the early years* (pp. 13–28). Sage Books.

Whitehead, A. N. (1938). *Modes of thought.* The Free Press.

(1920/2015). *The concept of nature.* Cambridge University Press.

Wilson, S. (2001). What is an indigenous research methodology? *Canadian Journal of Native Education, 25*(2), 240–255.

Wirihana, R. (2012). *Ngā pūrākau o ngā wāhine rangatira Māori o Aotearoa: The stories of Māori women leaders in New Zealand* (Unpublished PhD thesis). Massey University.

Woodhead, M. (1999). Reconstructing developmental psychology – some first steps. *Children & Society, 13*(1), 1–17. doi.org/10.1111/j.1099-0860.1999.tb00097.x

Index

kaupapa Màori Theory, 25–31
knowledge creation, 2

leaders, development of, 9, 76, 98
Leontiev, Aleksei, 98, 106–107

Màori, 19–20, 26, 42
  colonization. *See* Colonization
  effects of colonization (feelings of failure, loss,
    shame), 37–39, 52
  identity, 23
  Kaupapa Màori, 24–27, 38, 44–46, 48, 142
  women. *See* Wahine Màori
marginalization. *See* Racism
Marx, Karl, 11, 114
models of leadership, 1, 6, 20, 72
Murdoch, Iris, 148

Native Schools Act, 38
neo-liberalism, 12
New Zealand, 17, 20, 26, 28, 34–35, 38, 42, 51,
  See also Aotearoa
norway, 80

oppression, 20, 34, 36, 42, 44, 114

policy, 4, 6–8, 10, 13, 52, 139
professional development, 102–103, 135, 138
professionalism, reclaiming, 4
professionalization, 1, 5

qualification, 119, 122–123
quality, 1–2, 5, 8, 14, 49, 59, 85, 88, 103, 135,
  139, 141, 147
  crisis, 4, 8–10

racism, 39–42, 46
  marginalization, 17
  power, 41–42
  whiteness and white privilege. *See* Whiteness
    and white privilege
  responsibility, 4, 6–10, 14, 20, 94, 119, 130,
    140–141, 147
rhizome. *See* Writing

second in charge (2IC), 119
sedimentation, 113, 140
subjectivity, 4, 12, 64, 71–74, 139
supply. *See* Crisis

tangata whenua. *See* Màori
Te Ao Màori. *See* Màori
Te Ao Marama, 21
Te Reo Karanga o Matangireia, 23
Te Tiriti o Waitangi, 19–20, 26, 43, 52
Te Whāriki, 41
Think Tank Manifesto, 4–5
tikanga Màori principles, 31–34, 46, 49, 52
transformational pragmatics, 55, 58
Treaty of Waitangi. *See* Te Tiriti o Waitangi

Vygotsky, Lev, 98–99, 101–102

Wahine Màori, 17, 20, 23–24, 30, 38, 46
week stop meetings, 88–89
whiteness and white privilege, 6, 42–46
writing, 56–57
  Edupoetics, 68–71
  groups, 85, 88, 90, 93, 95
  organization concept, 67
  rhizomatic, 58–59, 61, 63–67, 76